CONTENTS

Ships in Focus Publications

Correspondence and editorial:
Roy Fenton
18 Durrington Avenue
London SW20 8NT
020 8879 3527
rfenton@rfenton.demon.co.uk

Orders and photographic:
John & Marion Clarkson
18 Franklands, Longton
Preston PR4 5PD
01772 612855
shipsinfocus@btinternet.com

Printed by Amadeus Press Ltd., Cleckheaton,
Yorkshire.
Designed by Hugh Smallwood, John
Clarkson and Roy Fenton.

SHIPS IN FOCUS RECORD
ISBN 978-1-901703-93-1

SUBSCRIPTION RATES FOR RECORD

Readers can start their subscription with
any issue, and are welcome to backdate it to
receive previous issues.

	3 issues	4 issues
UK	£24	£31
Europe (airmail)	£26	£34
Rest of the world (surface mail)	£26	£34
Rest of the world (airmail)	£31	£41

SHIPS IN FOCUS
November 2

With our interest in photographs, the publishers
that collectors now have fewer sources of 'new' prints from old, black and white
negatives. This situation has come about partly because of the difficulties of
obtaining dark room materials, and partly because of regulations on the disposal
of used photographic chemicals. Another factor is the time and skill required to
make 'real' photographic prints, which tend to make it uneconomic to produce
them on any scale.

Both Ships in Focus and John Clarkson personally have collections of
negatives built up over many years, the former comprising the negatives of British
and Commonwealth ships formerly belonging to Alex Duncan, which we bought
from his estate some years ago. With the development of digital imaging we have
decided to make offers of digital prints from these collections, the first of which
appears on the inside front cover of this issue. Initially we plan to make offers
available through 'Record' three times each year. However, if the orders warrant
it we may make more frequent offers, perhaps through our website or in other
publications. A further possibility is that other owners of collections may wish to
cooperate with us to make digital images available from their negatives.

It is important to note that the economical price quoted for digital copies
is only possible because the prints are produced in bulk. We have therefore
imposed a time limit of two months after publication for orders to be received:
those arriving later will be charged double. We are also prepared to produce
one-offs - prints from negatives not included in an offer - provided of course we
have a negative available. Owing to the time involved in locating and scanning
negatives, one-offs will be charged at a higher rate. Similarly, for prints larger
than the conventional postcard-size, a higher rate will be charged: details will be
provided on demand.

Customers should also note that this service is being run by a sister
company to Ships in Focus Publications, and payments should be made to Ships in
Focus Photographic.

We are pleased to say that we continue to receive high-quality material
for 'Record'. Together with some rather special features we have planned for our
fiftieth issue, due in November 2011, this means that – unless we have already
made a specific promise to the author –we cannot guarantee a slot for a new
article until well into 2012. In practice, this – plus our decision to change slightly
the balance of features in each issue – makes it more important than ever that
prospective authors contact us well before putting finger to keyboard.

John Clarkson   Roy Fenton

November 2010

Salford Corporation's *Salford* of 1895 arriving at Preston on 20th September
1928 for breaking up, having been bought by Thos.W. Ward Ltd. for £1,225.
[World Ship Society Ltd.]

Fleet in Focus

ELDER DEMPSTER POST WAR   Part 1

Andrew Bell

Elder Dempster had long dominated the trade route from Britain to the colonies in West Africa. It was not a long-haul route, for the passage time to the equatorial and primary port of Lagos, Nigeria took one of the company's mail boats only 12 days. However, it was a trade with unique challenges set in what had long been seen as an unhealthy climate: 'Beware of the Bight of Benin, where few come out of many who go in'.

Until the 1960s there were numerous lighterage ports, anchorages off nothing more than strips of sandy beaches. As if discharging and loading using surfboats was not challenging enough, there were the 'oil rivers', not yet associated with crude oil but ports at which vegetable oil seeds and oils were loaded. In the torpid rivers of the Niger River's delta ocean-going ships sailed 50 miles to ports set in mangrove forests. The master of the brand new *Sansu* (4,174grt) in 1939 had to cope with dubious anchorage holding grounds off a Gold Coast (later to become independent Ghana in 1957) surf port, with draught restrictions for crossing riverine bars plus 3,000 miles of coast line from Dakar to Lobito that offered almost no navigational aids and few natural harbours. Development in colonial countries was slow: Lagos Lagoon had been opened to sea-going ships only in 1916 and Takoradi's twin breakwaters, behind which a port was constructed, in 1928.

When the disruptive calamity of the Second World War started in September 1939 Elder Dempster's fleet comprised five passenger-cargo ships – the mail boats – and 34 cargo ships totalling 228,777grt. On all its routes the combined average annual cargo lift was neatly balanced at 550,000 freight tons southbound and the same tonnage northbound, carried on around 108 sailings, about 15 of which were trans-Atlantic between West Africa and the USA and Canada.

By the 1st January 1944 such had been the destruction of the fleet that there were only 15 of the pre-war ships left. Four of the five mailboats had been sunk leaving only the 26-year-old *Aba* (7,937/1918). Three ships had been bought from James Chambers during 1943. As a result of Alfred Holt's role in salvaging the wreckage and assets of the Kylsant empire there were close links between the companies and until 1943 direct management by Holts, which had provided the Caledon-built *Tarkwa* (7,416grt) in 1944 and Cammell Laird's standard type *Tamele* (7,172grt) in the same year. Substituting for the lost mail boats, each of the pair carried up to 40 passengers in spartan accommodation.

Into this bleak scene came John H. Joyce (1906-1982) as Managing Director and from 1946 until 1963 Chairman of the line. With extraordinary vision and talent, John Joyce - with the backing of (Sir) Alan Tod, Chairman of Elder Dempster's holding company - rapidly set about adding to the surviving fleet and also reconstructing the trade which even then was showing changes in the sources and destinations of cargoes. London and the South East began to equal Liverpool as the origin of exports. Hungry Britain also needed all the edible oils it could get and the post-war building boom took all the timber that West Africa could provide. To make the best use of all the shipping available the wartime arrangement of all the UK – West Africa Conference Lines' members' tonnage was combined into an operational pool. So satisfactory was this that

The Dundee-built *Tarkwa*, seen at anchor in the Thames in 1956, gave the company 23 years' service before being sold to Guan Guan (see 'The Last Grace') who renamed her *Golden Lion* in 1967. She was broken up at Shanghai in 1971. *[Roy Fenton collection]*

when de-controlled by the government in 1950 it remained, perpetuated, for much of rest of the 20th century. If one feature dominated John Joyce's management credo it was protecting and expanding Elder Dempster's pre-eminent position on all their trade routes. In one of his rare bellicose statements made in private to a management trainee in 1958, Joyce said that if necessary he would carry freight free to protect a sector of the company's business. Another Second World War development, the centralised purchase and onward sale of tropical produce by British state-controlled boards, was also maintained into peacetime and the boards' close contractual links with Elder Dempster were defended right up to 1962, ensuring stability and profitability.

The British Government was determined to eliminate the boom and bust seen in shipbuilding after the First World War and maintained control of scarce materials into the 1950s with a licence-to-build system. Having made a case to the ministries, licences enabled two mail boats to be ordered in February 1945 and a third one in March 1949. Action in 1945 to renew the cargo ship fleet included ordering six vessels from three UK shipbuilders: these were to become the new 'S' class. They were successors to five sister ships built between 1937 and 1939 which were smaller and to a different layout. The latter had been the first new buildings, apart from mail boat *Abosso* (11,330/1935), following the solution of the Kylsant debacle. Stately in appearance, they had a Blue Funnel

motor ship look about them. In the long superstructure the officers were accommodated at shelter deck level and the 12 passengers on the promenade deck. Number 3 hatch was trunked through the superstructure aft of the bridge. The war losses of the class all occurred in 1941 with the newest, *Seaforth*, sunk by *U 103* on 8th February, the *Swedru* (1) bombed in the Western Approaches on 16th April and the *Sangara* torpedoed at anchor off Accra by *U 69* on 30th May and sinking in the shallow roadstead. *Sangara* was enterprisingly salvaged and eventually repaired by the company's Wilmot Point engineering base after being bought from underwriters. The *Sobo* and *Sansu* were in the depleted fleet when the new 'S' class arrived from their builders' yards.

The new 'S' class
Ordering the six new ships was simplified by basing their hulls on the class of five built ten years previously. The hulls were longer by 19 feet at 407 feet and the depth to the shelter deck was the same at 33 feet. The important difference was increasing the beam by five feet to 57 feet in order to enhance stability. The fuller form of the hull increased the deadweight from 5,900 to 6,250 tons. The loaded draught at 22 feet meant that the ships of this class could sail, fully loaded, from any West African port except the trio in the Niger Delta – Sapele, Warri and Burutu. What may have helped was that Scotts had built three of the pre-

The Scotts-built *Sangara* (4,189/1939) had a remarkable career. Torpedoed by *U 69* whilst in Accra Roads in May 1941 she sank in 33 feet of water with the loss of her Master. Three months later the Italian submarine *Enrico Tazzoli* encountered the wreck and tried to torpedo it, but missed what must have been the ultimate sitting duck. In

April 1943 the underwriters to whom *Sangara* had been abandoned sold her for £500 to local interests who refloated and towed her first to Lagos Roads, then to Douala in the Cameroon. After her cargo had been sold, Elder Dempster repurchased her and at the end of the war their yard near Lagos made extensive repairs to both hull and

engines. In 1946 she was towed to South Shields for work to be completed, and began a second 'maiden' voyage from Liverpool on 10th April 1947. She was sold to breakers in 1960 and on 17th September arrived at Preston to be demolished by T.W. Ward Ltd. *[FotoFlite incorporating Skyfotos/J. and M. Clarkson collection]*

Sherbro of 1947. *[Ships in Focus/Roy Fenton collection]*

war five and were able to accept orders for three of the post-war six. Such was the competition for available building berths that orders went to two builders never before used by Elder Dempster, Furness (two ships) and Hawthorn Leslie (one).

In appearance the second 'S' class were practical rather than elegant. Three decks were topped by the bridge, forward on the midships block of accommodation. In the days before the performance of air conditioning was safe and dependable, shaded areas dominated the design: each deck had a promenade deck around it. This was unkindly described by some observers as giving the new 'S' class the look of a plate of sandwiches. Number 3 hatch was now at the after end of the fore deck.

A number of other features reflected the needs of the West African trade. In the number 1 lower 'tween deck were four permanent timber lockers for explosives with the detonators being stowed at the after extremity of the hull in a small locker under the poop. Arranged athwartships in number 3 hold were six separate deep tanks each with a capacity of 160 tonnes. When carrying palm oil the tanks were heated by steam coils and whenever possible were used only for northbound stems of oil because handling break-bulk general cargo in them was slow and risked damaging the cargo and the coils. Three masts and one pair of derrick posts were used for heavily-scantlinged derricks which could meet the challenges of handling hardwood logs. There was a heavy-lift derrick with a safe working load of 50 tonnes that served number 2 hatch, the largest hold of all: this derrick was useful for heavy items of capital equipment. All the electric winches were standard production models from Laurence Scott.

Even though Elder Dempster operated passenger ships, accommodation was supplemented by 12 berths on most of the cargo ships. It was one of the trends in the post-war building boom that many cargo ships – even tramps

– were provided with accommodation for 12 passengers. The new 'S' class were no exception, for on the first deck above the shelter deck were located eight single and two double cabins with a lounge at the forward end and a large airy verandah at the after end. Contemporary cabin plans show a single cabin for a stewardess but it is thought that this was only ever used for members of the company's large European staff running the offices in West Africa. On the shelter deck forward was the dining saloon used by all the officers and passengers. The main galley was adjacent, aft of the saloon. A poop on two decks meant that all the West African ratings had two-berth cabins: all the mess rooms were amidships. In the forecastle there was a covered area for inter-coastal African deck passengers with a small galley and six lavatories: their custom was an important part of the pattern of trade, usually they carried large quantities of trade goods.

The favourite way of reducing port dues in 1947-1948 was to have the upper deck open for the length of all the cargo spaces from number 1 to 5 holds with only a small amount of reefer cargo lockers (two), ship's stores space and the engine casing intruding into it.

The class was powered by four-cylinder standard Doxford diesel engines producing 3,200 BHP and giving a service speed of 12.5 knots on 15 tonnes of fuel a day.

In service

The new 'S' class came into service not a day too soon for there was a pent-up demand for goods in the British colonies of West Africa as a result of wartime shortages. From wealthy cocoa farmers on the (then) Gold Coast to feudal chieftains in Northern Nigeria, there was a demand for everything that was new, from electrical appliances to luxury cars. The consignments of staple commodities such as ICI's bagged salt and Tate & Lyle's refined sugar were 'bottom stow' cargo on every southbound sailing. But the largest commodity of all was bagged cement from Blue Circle's huge plant at Northfleet on the Thames: loading might start there and finish across the Thames at Tilbury.

In the northbound direction oil seeds to produce fats for food-rationed Britain had priority. Coming ever more to the fore was the timber trade: tropical logs sawn for rebuilding and refurnishing war-damaged Britain. One shift in the pattern of the trade was how the growth of shipments through Tilbury challenged the once-dominant position of Glasgow and Liverpool. Whilst stevedoring in British terminal ports had its problems these were as nothing compared to those in West Africa where conditions ranged from modern alongside quays in Takoradi and Lagos (Apapa) to the surf ports of Accra, Winneba and Cape Coast. In Nigeria and Sierra Leone Elder Dempster's large fleet of lighters and tugs were the means for cargo handling and distribution in the Niger Delta ports, Calabar, and Victoria (West Cameroon).

The quest for US dollars earned by West African exports and the demand for US and Canadian milled flour meant that it was not long before the new 'S' class were seen on the company's long-established trans-Atlantic route. In spite of the allure of the lavish lifestyles in North America these sailings were not popular with officers for it meant extended periods away from home shores, particularly if the ship was programmed to make more than one round voyage. Sea staff joined the company for short voyages not long ones. These were the days long before wives and families accompanied sea staff. Another long-established cross trade was carrying Ghanaian hardwood to South Africa and returning with supplies for the Ashanti gold mines.

Even John Joyce's prescient going-for-growth policy was challenged by the increase in the volumes of cargoes. In ten years between 1946 and 1956 the West African trade had grown from 7,000,000 to 75,000,000 tons. To keep their share of this expansion Elder Dempster

became major charterers of ships, notably during the tropical produce export season from November through to April. Amongst the ships supplementing the 'S' class were the 'K's, general-purpose tramps mainly built by Lithgows for a subsidiary of Henderson Line of Glasgow. So established did this business link become that, lead by the Borland family, their company accepted a £6,000,000 cash offer (all but 6% of which was paid from Elder Dempster's own reserves) and this permanently added six ships to the fleet with another five on order and, of course, four ships on Henderson's long-established trade to Burma, Ceylon, and the Sudan which was shared with Bibby Line. In 1946 five Canadian 'Fort and Park' type standard ships had been bought, originally by Elder Dempster (Canada) Ltd., and in 1947, three 'Liberty' ships.

John Holt were long-established Liverpool merchants with a series of import-export trading ventures in West Africa and a modest river transport fleet based at Warri and plying the Niger River. John Holt had since 1907 carried their own cargo in their own ships but in 1950 they joined the Freight Conference and formed Guinea Gulf Line which usually operated four ships. Oddly, the company never owned a diesel-powered ocean-going ship and their new buildings were always steam propelled. After an attempt was made to sell Guinea Gulf to the young Nigerian National Shipping Line, Elder Dempster bought the company in 1965 with its Conference rights and its four ships. As soon as the purchase was effected the steamers were sold with one exception – and that was for just one round voyage. None of the ships appeared in West Africa as units of the Elder Dempster fleet. The direct result of the disposal was that all six of the new 'S' class were transferred to Guinea Gulf Line with their yellow funnels painted in the John Holt colours of red with a black top. All six 'S' names were replaced by those of places in West Africa beginning with 'M', none of which had previously been used by

Cambray (7,209/1944) sailing from Swansea, one of five 'Fort and Park' type ships bought in 1946. The former *Bridgeland Park* she was sold in 1960 to Swiss owners and renamed *Simeto*. She was broken up at Bilbao in 1971. *[Roy Fenton collection]*

Like other liner companies, Elder Dempster bought a clutch of Liberties in 1947. *Zungon* (7,267/1943), formerly *Samyale*, was one of the three purchased in 1947 and is seen here at Cape Town in December 1954. She was sold in 1968. *[Ships in Focus]*

Elder Dempster. John Holt's sea staff had been absorbed into T. and J. Brocklebank when they were awarded the management contract of the Guinea Gulf quartet a few years previously. The Elder Dempster purchase ended this when the Ocean Group's Ocean Fleets took over. There had been an amalgamation of Blue Funnel and Elder Dempster in 1965 with an agreed takeover of the latter's holding company, Liner Holdings: in the process Ocean Transport and Trading was formed, a publicly quoted company.

It had long been a tenet of Elder Dempster's strategic policy that, together with their relevant Conference partners, they would carry all the cargo offering to and from

British West Africa. This trade was nibbled away at by a succession of non-Conference lines, but there was no serious challenge until Comecon ships appeared in 1962, those of Polska Zegluga Morska of Poland. There was a defiant stand by the UK and national Conference lines particularly to protect the UK trade and even in the cock-eyed world of Communist-style voyage accounting, PZM's losses could not be sustained for long. In this campaign the new 'S' class played a substantial role in acting as 'sweepers', carriers of small parcels of cargo to and from secondary ports, be it loading railway lines at Middlesbrough, Dunlop's plantation's rubber at Calabar, Rose's lime juice off Cape

Sulima was renamed *Mano* from February 1965 to her sale in June 1967. She was photographed in May 1966. *[Ships in Focus]*

Coast or piassava (the bristles for brooms) at Sherbro. The Ocean Group's chairman, Sir John N. Nicholson, was not convinced that this defensive strategy was worthwhile, for it produced financial losses. On a visit to Lagos in 1967 he made an imperial edict and the 'S' cum 'M' class were disposed of almost there and then, despite having played an important and profitable role for 20 years.

Enter the 'E' class

The design of the new 'S' class was a stopgap one: getting ships ordered, built and into service was the priority. From the in-house naval architects a new shape was seen when the *Eboe* emerged from Scotts in March 1952. She and her identical sister ship *Ebani* were almost the largest cargo ships built for the company since a trio in 1923-1924: they were prestige ships ordered specifically for the USA-West Africa-Congo trade. From the same drawing board came the third mail boat *Aureol*. There were similarities in the details, seen in companionways merged into visually pleasing, often curved superstructure, airy public rooms across the forward end of the centre castle on the 'E's, hidden working alleyways, and a sleek silhouette which some saw as equal to the ships being built at the same time for Silver Line, Port Line and Dodero.

In spacious accommodation on the promenade deck there were two double-berth passenger cabins and eight singles, each with private facilities that included full-sized bath tubs. Another feature never repeated in the fleet was that the four cadets were housed in a genuine halfdeck (house) on the boat deck: in this penthouse position they were out of sight, out of mind and could make as much noise as they wanted to.

After what appeared to be satisfactory acceptance trials the *Eboe* loaded a full general cargo in Liverpool for West Africa and sailed on 15th March 1952 only to experience a major breakdown of her six-cylinder 8,000 BHP Scott-Doxford diesel main engine so serious that she returned to Liverpool, discharged the complete cargo and went back to the builders where she was worked on for three months.

According to Donald H. Tod (1929-2009), an Elder Dempster Assistant Manager who as personal assistant to John Joyce was held by many to have the best shipping brain in India Buildings, there was board level disquiet about the two new 'E's. They were ordered before the much larger and more complex flagship (*Aureol* from Alexander Stephens), were delivered later and cost as much. It is thought that this is why the third ship of the class built by Scotts was changed to become the very basic economy type, *Patani* (6,183/1954). With her sister ship *Perang* (6,177/1954) coming from William Gray, Elder Dempster had two ships for the total cost of one 'E'. This undistinguished pair are remembered as being so 'schooner rigged' that the main galley could not produce toast if the cargo winches were working.

Once in service it was soon apparent that the two 'E' class were too valuable on the mainline service between the UK and West Africa to be employed cross trading with the USA, Canada and Africa. Although long having been one-third owned by Elder Dempster, the Belgian CMB line kept the lucrative Congo trade to itself. The use to which the 'E's were particularly suited was as two of the ships in the fortnightly express service between Tilbury, Dakar, Lagos (Customs Wharf) and Port Harcourt taking in Ghana ports northbound and perhaps Abidjan. In service they were over a knot faster than the mail boats and there was said to be a company rule that they were only to overtake the passenger ships below the horizon by day or under the cover of darkness. The eventual third ship of the class was ordered

First of the 'E' class, *Eboe* with substantial deck cargo. *[FotoFlite incorporating Skyfotos/J. and M. Clarkson collection]*

from Scotts in 1955, and delivered in February 1957. She was the *Egori* and was different from the two earlier ships in having no passenger accommodation in her tall, centralised block of superstructure. The ship was powered by one of Doxford's first turbo-charged engines that produced 9,000 BHP. Another new feature were the four bipod masts with heavily-geared derricks and winches serving six hatches all on one level. In the late 1960s the *Egori* was the chosen ship to trial the first cargo containers in the West African trade. Yet another first was a system that eliminated heating coils in the two deep tanks, each with a capacity of 544 tonnes, that piped the palm oil into a heating system in the nearby engine room and recirculated it to the deep tanks. So successful was this that it was repeated in every other cargo ship the company had built after the *Egori* proved that the simplicity of the system worked: it was another unsung achievement and it could not be patented.

[To be continued]

SHERBRO/MATRU

Furness Shipbuilding Co. Ltd., Haverton Hill-on-Tees, 1947; 4,811gt, 408 feet 4-cyl. 2SCSA Doxford-type oil engine by Richardsons, Westgarth and Co. Ltd., Hartlepool.
Sherbro was launched on 10th May 1947 by Mrs W.L. Robinson, the wife of an Elder Dempster director. The upper photograph shows her in 1955.

Seen in the lower photograph in May 1966, *Matru*, as she became on transfer to Guinea Gulf Line Ltd. with the rest of the 'S' class in 1965, raised £100,000 when sold in 1967, and became the Cyprus-registered *Agia Eftychia*, ultimate owners being P.A. Lemos and Associates, or at least their finance house.

In 1971 she was sold to a company ostensibly based in Somalia, and renamed *Moka*. Beneficial owner was M.A. Panjwani of London, but he was probably acting for shipbreakers, as on 28th November of that year *Moka* arrived at Karachi where United Shipbreaking Industries were to break her up. *[J. and M. Clarkson; Ships in Focus]*

SHONGA/MALLAM

Scotts' Shipbuilding and Engineering Co. Ltd., Greenock, 1947; 4,810gt, 408 feet

4-cyl. 2SCSA Doxford-type oil engine by Scotts' Shipbuilding and Engineering Co. Ltd., Greenock

On 19th August 1947 *Shonga* was sponsored by Mrs C.T.J. Cripps, the wife of another Elder Dempster director, who was a close relative of the then Chancellor of the Exchequer, Sir Stafford Cripps. The top photograph shows *Shonga* on the Thames.

In their book 'The Elder Dempster Fleet History 1852-1985', James Cowden and John Duffy note that *Shonga* was the only member of the 'S' class to have her name painted on her white 'half-rounds' rather than the black of her hull. The photographs in this feature tend to confirm this observation.

Shonga was renamed *Mallam* on transfer to Guinea Gulf Line in April 1965, but when photographed (middle) on 16th July 1967 she had reverted to Elder Dempster's funnel colours. Judging from her berth, she was probably laid up awaiting sale.

When sold on 25th November 1967 she also raised £100,000, going to Pacific International Lines (Pte.) Ltd. of Singapore for whom she became *Kota Maju*. In the final photograph she is anchored off Singapore on 16th July 1977. She still appears to be working cargo, but just over three months later, and after almost ten years under the Singapore flag, she arrived at Gadani Beach on 31st October 1977 to be broken up by Sharfaq Industrial. *[W.H. Brown/Roy Fenton collection; J. and M. Clarkson (2)]*

SALAGA/MAMFE

Hawthorn, Leslie and Co. Ltd.,
Newcastle-upon-Tyne, 1947; 4,810gt,
408 feet
4-cyl. 2SCSA Doxford-type oil engine
by Hawthorn, Leslie and Co. Ltd.,
Newcastle-upon-Tyne

When launched on 18th June 1947,
Salaga was named by Mrs J.G. Beazley,
wife of a non-executive director of Elder
Dempster.

As *Mamfe* she became the
last of the class to be owned by the
company, not sold until 9th February
1968 when she raised £115,000.
Initially owners were Welcome Shipping
Co. Ltd. and as *Lucky Trader* she
remained registered at Liverpool. Later
in 1968, however, she was transferred
to Singapore Shipping Development
Co. Private Ltd. who registered her in
Singapore.

Lucky Trader was sold to China
for scrapping and arrived at Hsinkang
on 12th March 1973. However, a vessel
of this class was photographed at Hong
Kong in 1982 under the Chinese flag,
and this was almost certainly the former
Salaga. Her fate is unknown.

She is shown at each stage
in her career: as *Salaga* in the Thames
on 15th March 1953 still with white
forecastle and poop (top), as *Mamfe*
whilst on charter to erstwhile rival
Chargeurs Reunis in 1965 (middle),
and as *Lucky Trader* in the Straits of
Malacca (bottom). [*Ships in Focus*
(2); Airfoto of Malacca/Roy Fenton
collection]

SEKONDI/MAMPONG

*Furness Shipbuilding Co. Ltd.,
Haverton Hill-on-Tees, 1948;
4,811gt, 408 feet
4-cyl. 2SCSA Doxford-type oil
engine by Richardsons, Westgarth
and Co. Ltd., Hartlepool.*
The sponsor at the launch of
Sekondi on 17th June 1947 was
Mrs Marion Smye, wife of the
Company Secretary.

The middle photograph of
Sekondi was taken off Cape Town
in March 1957.

As *Mampong* (bottom,
once more in Elder Dempster's
funnel colours) she was sold on
22nd September 1967 to the
Peseta Shipping Corporation
S.A. of Panama, controlled by the
Everett Steamship Corporation of
Manila, who renamed her *Java
Sea*. In 1968 Hong Kong's Quincy
Chuang acquired her and renamed
her *Fortune Carrier*, swapping her
Panama flag for that of the Somali
Republic. A further sale in July of
the same year saw the ultimate
owner become the Far East
Corporation Ltd. of Singapore.

Fortune Carrier did not
live up to her name and became
the shortest lived of the 'S'
class. On 1st October 1968 she
foundered during a typhoon off
Swatow in position 23.02 north,
116.33 east during a voyage
from Hong Kong to Hsinkang,
China with a cargo of scrap iron.
*[Fotoflite incorporating Skyfotos;
Ships in Focus; David Whiteside
collection]*

SULIMA/MANO

Scotts' Shipbuilding and Engineering Co. Ltd., Greenock, 1948; 4,810gt, 408 feet
4-cyl. 2SCSA Doxford-type oil engine by Scotts' Shipbuilding and Engineering Co. Ltd., Greenock
Mrs A.M. Bennett, wife of Elder Dempster's Technical Director, launched *Sulima* on 27th January 1948.

The top photograph of *Sulima* was probably take at Tilbury. In the upper middle photograph, believed to have been taken by Robert Moffat Scott, she approaches Cape Town in 1955. The ships were occasional visitors to South Africa with timber from Ghana, and might return with mining supplies and equipment.

As *Mano* (lower middle, in Guinea Gulf funnel colours) she fetched £115,000 on 26th June 1967 when Frangos Brothers and Co. bought her and put her under the Greek flag as *Anna F* (bottom).

Her career was cut short by engine damage, sustained in March 1972. After lying in Antwerp until September 1973 she was towed to Gdansk, but the Polish yard proved unable to repair her economically. She then set out for breakers in Bilbao, again under tow, but on 4th December 1973 broke adrift off Klaipeda and stranded in position 54.58 north, 20.17 east. *[Roy Fenton collection; Ships in Focus; J. and M. Clarkson; Airfoto of Malacca/Roy Fenton collection]*

SWEDRU/MARADI

Scotts' Shipbuilding and Engineering Co. Ltd., Greenock, 1948; 4,809gt, 408 feet

4-cyl. 2SCSA Doxford-type oil engine by Richardsons, Westgarth and Co. Ltd., Hartlepool.

The last member of the class was launched on 22nd April 1948 by Mrs J.H. Joyce, wife of Elder Dempster's Chairman. *Swedru* is seen in the upper photograph in May 1953, and as *Maradi* in Guinea Gulf colours in the middle shot.

Maradi was sold on 19th June 1967 to Kollakis Brothers of Piraeus who initially put her under the Greek flag as *Kabalaris* (bottom). In 1968 this was swapped for the anaemic-looking flag of Cyprus, although without change of registered owner, Kavalaris Shipping Co. Ltd., Famagusta. On 7th June 1972 *Kabalaris* arrived at Bilbao and in August of that year Revalorizacion de Materiales S.A. began to demolish her. *[J. and M. Clarkson; World Ship Society Ltd.; Roy Fenton collection]*

EBOE

Scotts' Shipbuilding and Engineering Co. Ltd., Greenock, 1952; 9,397gt, 508 feet 6-cyl. 2SCSA Doxford-type oil engine by Scotts' Shipbuilding and Engineering Co. Ltd., Greenock

On 19th September 1951 *Eboe* was named and launched by Lady Milverton, wife of Lord Milverton, the Governor General of Nigeria (1943-1948), perhaps the highest profile sponsor of any of the ships featured here.

At some point in their careers, the radar mast on the bridges of *Eboe* and *Ebani* were extended in height and repainted from white into 'mast' colour. Photos also show that forecastles and poops were later repainted black, with the ships' names appearing higher on the forecastle.

After a satisfyingly long, 25-year career with Elder Dempster, *Eboe* was sold on 19th September 1977 to the Liberian-registered Triton Navigation Corporation, managed by Maldives Shipping Ltd., and renamed *Georgios*. In 1978 she was transferred to the parent company, Maldives Shipping Ltd., her name modified to *Georgia* and the Liberian flag gave way to that of Panama. This was probably for just one voyage, as on 19th February 1978 she arrived at Gadani Beach where the breakers began work on her almost at once. *[J.K. Byass/World Ship Society Ltd.]*

EBANI

Scotts' Shipbuilding and Engineering Co. Ltd., Greenock, 1952; 9,396gt, 508 feet 6-cyl. 2SCSA Doxford-type oil engine by Scotts' Shipbuilding and Engineering Co. Ltd., Greenock

Seen here in 1957, *Ebani's* career was extremely simple. She was launched and named on 13th March 1952 by Miss J. Tod, daughter of Sir Alan Tod, chairman of Elder Dempster's holding company. In 1953 *Ebani* was transferred to the China Mutual Steam Navigation Co. Ltd. for a single round voyage to the Far East before reverting to Elder Dempster ownership. It can be assumed that she wore a regulation blue funnel for this voyage. On 15th August 1977 she arrived at Faslane to be broken up by Shipbreaking Industries Ltd. *[World Ship Society Ltd.]*

EGORI

Scotts' Shipbuilding and Engineering Co. Ltd., Greenock, 1957; 9,586gt, 509 feet
6-cyl. 2SCSA Doxford-type oil engine by Scotts' Shipbuilding and Engineering Co. Ltd., Greenock

Launched on 12th January 1956, *Egori* was sponsored by Lady Hobhouse, wife of Sir John Hobhouse, a partner in Alfred Holt.

On virtually the same dimensions as *Eboe* and *Ebani*, the *Egori* appeared very different, and with her bipod masts presaged the much smaller 'F' class. She too gave the company excellent service, with her Elder Dempster ownership again broken by transfer to China Mutual for a single voyage in 1972. The lower photograph from 5th June 1975 shows that she was also painted in Guinea Gulf colours. As with *Eboe* and *Ebani*, a taller radar mast was fitted mid-career (although painted white), and black paint extended higher on the hull.

Sale on 6th September 1978 saw her, unusually, going to Kuwait owners in the shape of Ali Khalifa Mirchandani Shipping Co. Ltd. who renamed her *Azza*. Once again, Elder Dempster had got the most out of her, and just over a year later, on 9th October 1979, *Azza* arrived at Kaohsiung having been sold for demolition to Li Chong Iron Works Co. Ltd. *[J.K. Byass/World Ship Society Ltd.; World Ship Society Ltd.]*

THE LAST MEETING
John Clarkson

The Preston yard of Thomas W. Ward closed in the early 1970s and towards the end the ships handled became smaller and smaller to the extent that we eventually saw little more than dumb barges from the Mersey. The last decent-sized ships to be broken up were Elders and Fyffes' *Tilapa* (5,401/1928) which arrived on 8th June 1959, *Sangara* on 17th September 1960, *Aase Maersk* (6,185/1930) on 20th December 1960 and finally *Sansu* on 20th January 1961.

    Tilapa took ages to demolish due to the amount of cork insulation in her and which resulted in frequent fires onboard. *Sanagra* must have been lightened very quickly and moved on to the grid as A*ase Maersk* went directly to the breaking berth. Between these ships various trawlers and coasters were dealt with, most of which would go straight on the grid. Above we see *Sangara* on Ward's berth soon after arrival. The second photo was taken from part way up the coal conveyor bridge. Although there were proper steps and handrails, access would be denied these days on safety grounds.

As *Sansu* arrived she would pass the stripped down *Sangara* on the grid and *Aase Maersk* on the berth. She then went under the bridge which carried the power station coal conveyor and was put on the eastern end of the New Diversion Quay to await her turn (top). Several months later and when the shipbreaking berth was clear for her, tugs would have made fast, her lines slackened off and as the tide started to ebb she would be allowed to almost drift down river by not much more than her length on to the breaking berth (middle). The same procedure would be followed when her time came to move on to the gridiron for final demolition. Smaller ships were sometimes moved without any tug assistance, using only the tide and man-power. In the final picture demolition has commenced, removing masts and other top hamper and her funnel has been felled and lies on her accomodation block.

Only one further decent-sized ship came to Preston for scrapping, Thompson's *Sithonia* (7,123/1942), completed as the *Ocean Volga*. She arrived on 18th December 1961 from Liverpool but that's another story.

THE LAST GRACE or SILVER INTO GOLD
Captain A.W. Kinghorn

By the 1970s the last of the Liberties were being replaced. Any ship approaching thirty years old must pass such rigorous surveys that the cost of keeping her in class usually exceeds that which she can be expected to earn in her future life. Steam reciprocating engines had become outdated with spares expensively hard to find. Steelwork was wearing out. The last Liberties had to go. But despite the container revolution and the tendency to build bigger and bigger single-deck bulk carriers, there was - and perhaps always will be - a limited demand for handy-sized, two-deck dry cargo ships, able to carry break-bulk cargo and/or containers from and to the world's less sophisticated, shallow-draught ports. Sunderland's SD14, of which 211 were built, was one of the most successful replacements. Germany had their version of a two-deck, 15,000-ton deadweight, 15-knot ship, known simply as the Liberty Replacement, two vessels of which type I commanded when they themselves were in their twenties. They were good ships which compared well with their Sunderland rivals, although the Germans had a poor double-bottom tank pumping system while to me the SD14 often seemed underpowered. The Japanese were building their utilitarian Freedom classes and also a less numerous class, the MM14. In all these classes the bulbous bow was an optional extra while final layout was usually left to the owners who paid for it all, resulting in some of each class being better than others. Two of these MM14s, built at Hiroshima by Mitsubishi during 1976-77, were the last vessels for the British Silver Line, subtitled Silverdee Shipping Ltd. of London. These were the *Silverdee* and *Silveravon*.

Foreign ownership

But this was the time when the once-great British Merchant Navy was going into terminal decline and these two ships were soon sold. *Silveravon* became *Bandama* in 1978, *Enarxis* in 1985 and *Trade Grace* in 1988. Chartered to Guan Guan, she was found to be ideally suited to their mainline service from China to the Middle East and was, at the end of this charter, bought outright, becoming *Golden Grace*. Thus, in 1994, that old alchemists' dream came true - silver was converted into gold.

An elegant vessel with nicely rounded cruiser stern, raised poop deck on which stood the funnel and accommodation block, four cargo hatches (two of which were paired double) ending with a handsome raised forecastle. For a ship built in 1977 she was unusual in that her rounded clipper stem lacked the bulb which, since the early 1960s, has become standard for nearly every class of ship. In those early years a great deal was written about the 'scientifically test-tank proven' advantages of this new bulbous bow - how its design enabled a ship to save fuel by lessening water resistance by making a streamlined entrance.

Having sailed deep sea for 47 years (including ten times round the world, in a total of 23 ships without bulbs and eight with) I am left in no doubt as to which makes a better sea boat in heavy weather. When pitching into a heavy swell the bulb is so streamlined that your ship dives straight through it with the heavy water coming aboard, potentially doing immense damage to your ship. Whereas a well-flared non-bulbous bow rides gracefully over the waves with little water coming aboard, safer and more comfortable

Silveravon of 1977, later to become Guan Guan's *Golden Grace*. *[David Whiteside collection]*

Golden Grace in Guan Guan ownership. Funnel and masts are blue. *[David Whiteside collection]*

- always provided you are not driving her too hard! In the unfortunate event of a collision, a bulbous-bowed ship, deep laden, striking another ship, holes her well below the waterline. I saw two ships thus in the Shanghai River in 1989. The bulb had effectively torpedoed the other ship just abaft amidships, impaling both on a convenient sandbank.

    Golden Grace's main machinery was a five-cylinder Sulzer of 7,500 BHP (5,517 kw) which originally gave a speed of 15 knots now, with her aged 20, it was little better than 12. Gross tonnage was 10,869 on a length of 151.1 metres, beam 22.1 metres. All deck machinery was hydraulic, more of which later. Single Velle swinging derricks worked her general cargo in and out in ports where

no shore cranes were available. The small crane amidships between hatches 2 and 3 had never been satisfactory and was never used. A similar midships crane in MM14 sister ship *Golden Wonder*, when I was in her five years earlier, had been removed and lay rusting away on a Shanghai quayside. A heavy-lift derrick capable of working cargo at hatches 3 and 4 was also disused, having run out of class. On this trade it was not deemed necessary.

    Guan Guan - which means in Chinese 'continually flowing water', also 'continually flowing gold' (as water flows past our ships, gold flows into our company coffers), was, hence, The Golden Line. The owners, Thios, were an old Chinese Indonesian family who had done well in

Golden Wonder, a sister of *Golden Grace*, built in 1969 as *Corviglia*. *[V.H. Young and L.A. Sawyer]*

business when Indonesia was still the Dutch East Indies. The company's efforts in no small way helped their country obtain independence from the Netherlands and after independence in December 1949 the family further prospered, with several small ships carrying their produce inter island while newly purchased second-hand vessels extended trade further afield. But despite being blessed with much fertile land, vast timber resources, sea fisheries and minerals waiting to be mined, Indonesia remained impoverished, partly due, no doubt, to widescale corruption in high places. President Sukarno endeavoured to increase his personal wealth by initiating a policy now known as ethnic cleansing. His wealthy, hardworking Chinese subjects became his victims, so for the good of their health the Thio family moved lock stock and barrel to Singapore, taking their ships with them.

But they remained loyal - as the Chinese do - and continued to employ Indonesian seamen. It was Mr Thio's ambition to own fifty ships, including cargo passenger liners and he nearly made it, sadly succumbing to cancer shortly before he attained this ambition. His widow handed the company over to her three grown-up children, British-educated and well fitted to bring the company into modern times. Realising that the container revolution was rapidly putting their old-style shipping out of date - no longer could a small company's ships pick up lucrative cargoes around the world on chance - they wisely retrenched, selling off the smaller ships and concentrated on buying cargo liners of around 9,000 gross tons, placing them on what had always been their main trade, between China and the Middle East. When the Communists finally achieved government over all China in 1949, proclaiming the People's Republic, the USA and British governments 'officially' ceased trading with them (except through Hong Kong), hoping in this way to bring the Communists down. Of all the non-Chinese shipping companies who formerly traded with China, only two refused to give up. One was the German Rickmers Line, the other Guan Guan.

Ultimately surviving these western bans, the Chinese government subsequently allowed only these two foreign companies to set up services from and to China, with the result that Guan Guan developed a monthly cargo liner service to the Middle East. Around the 27th of each month a Golden Line ship would sail from Shanghai with a full general cargo for Singapore, Colombo, Karachi, Dubai, Damman and Kuwait, with full cargoes of urea fertiliser assured for the trip back east. Most of these urea cargoes, in bag or bulk, were for Chinese ports, but sometimes for Colombo, Bangkok or the Philippines and occasionally it was possible to fit in a cross cargo such as sugar from Bangkok to Japan or fertiliser from the Philippines to China, provided the monthly loading from Shanghai could be achieved. Interesting!

Eastern ways
When I joined Guan Guan in June 1988 they had the Dutch-built *Golden Haven*, a conventional cargo vessel built 1964 as the *London Advocate* for Basil Mavroleon's London and Overseas Freighters, *Golden Wonder*, a Shimonoseki MM14 built in 1969, plus *Golden Harvest* and *Golden Bear*, both German Liberty Replacements of 1970 from Rickmers of Bremerhaven and from Flensburg, respectively. Later they bought another German Liberty, *Golden Star*, and became interested in an SD14 which had come up for sale. My wife was asked to obtain SD14 plans from Newcastle's Discovery Museum which she did, and the ship was surveyed in Singapore by the company superintendents with great interest. But the ship - less than 20 years old - had been shamefully neglected by her previous owners and was found to be well past it. Conveniently, *Golden Grace* came along, by which time *Golden Wonder* and *Golden Haven* had also been sold. With only four vessels operating a four-month round voyage this tight loading schedule meant that occasionally outside ships, usually Chinese, had to be chartered in. Eventually the *Golden Grace* was their last and only ship.

Bought in 1984, *Golden Haven* had been built at Vlissingen in 1965 as *London Advocate*. *[World Ship Society Ltd.]*

Two of the three German Liberty Replacements owned by Guan Guan. Acquired in 1988, *Golden Bear* (top and middle) had been launched at Flensburg as *Martha Fisser* but was completed in 1970 as *Sunbaden*. *Golden Star* (bottom) was completed by Bremer Vulkan A.G. at Vegesack as *Lumumba* in 1974, later carrying the names *Labrador* and *Pace* before being bought by Guan Guan in 1991. [*World Ship Society Ltd.; Ian J. Farquhar; V.H. Young and L.A. Sawyer*]

Golden Bear crossing the Bay of Bengal in a south west monsoon. *[Author]*

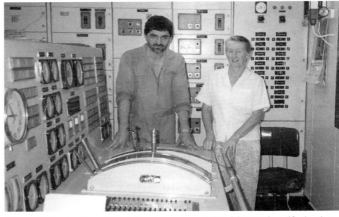

Blazo Milovic, the Chief Engineer, and the Master's wife in the engine control room of the *Golden Grace* on 15th March 1997. *[Author]*

Part of *Golden Bear's* deck cargo in January 1996. *[Author]*

Blazo and the author relaxing with a drink on board *Golden Grace*. *[Author]*

The Burmese radio officer. *[Author]*

Discharging urea from the *Golden Harvest* at Wujin, a port up-river from Shanghai, in April 1992. *[Author]*

Mess room party on *Golden Grace* in 1997. *[Author]*

Last Grace

After eight years with this interesting, well-run family company, I had five months leave before flying out on 27th August 1996 to join *Golden Grace* in Singapore's Eastern Roads two days later, as she came to anchor in pouring rain. I was pleased to find here my old Indonesian Chief Officer Hasan Meliala from Medan, Sumatra, with whom I had sailed previously in *Golden Wonder* and *Golden Harvest*. The Second Mate too was an old shipmate - Christian Steven Pattiasina, also Indonesian, from Jakarta. He had demonstrated to me what an excellent Second Mate he was in *Golden Harvest*. A small, well-run, tightly knit company like Guan Guan kept its best men for years, in all departments - and with tours of duty for all hands of at least one year, more if they so wished - we all got to know and appreciate each other. Such an atmosphere onboard makes for the greatest efficiency in running a ship - all hands know what has to be done and get on with it, cheerfully and wholeheartedly. Our full complement of 29 included Indonesians, Burmese, Malaysians, Chinese, Philippinos, occasionally Ghanese and Nigerians and, latterly, men from that part of Jugoslavia known as Montenegro.

When, on 21st June 1992, the United Nations placed sanctions on Jugoslavia, their entire merchant navy was immediately laid up at ports around the world. Their men had to seek work elsewhere to maintain families and homes and some came to Guan Guan. The engineers in particular were exceptionally good - knowledgeable, concientious and hard working. Their English was improving all the time. The Chief and Second Engineers in the *Golden Grace*, Blazo and Peter, had been old schoolmates, served their apprenticeships together, done their national service together in the Jugoslav Navy - but this was the first big ship in which they had sailed together. They and Hasan the Mate got on famously and it is a fact that if you and your senior officers get on well together you have all the makings of a well run, happy ship. They got her speed up to 14.5 knots from an average 12 on considerably less fuel consumption than before they came and even got the long-disused air conditioning to work perfectly. Real engineers!

I - and my wife when she came with me - were the only two Brits onboard, but fortunately English remains the international language of the sea, though of course we picked up snatches of all our shipmates' tongues as a matter of courtesy - which also helped the ship run smoothly. My wife was known as 'Auntie', which she rather liked, and in Karachi she was 'Memsahib' - even better!

The Real World

I began to realise in Guan Guan that my two years on HMS *Conway* followed by 37 years in Blue Star Line had been a good apprenticeship for life in the Real World, as this certainly was. I was able to help in many ways, using my experience of general cargo work, navigation, ship maintenance and - very importantly - shipmaster's business. This subject had been part of my master's certificate exam nearly 35 years ago but in a British liner company most shipmaster's business was conducted by office staff and agents around the world, who dealt with most of the cargo and all the other legal papers so necessary in running a ship. Here I found most of it was up to me. When port authorities and other crooked shore officials applied their wiles in attempts to embezzle me and my employers, I had to learn how to outwit them - and it was a sombre fact that a smart white uniform with an English voice helped in this respect. Worldwide, port papers, cargo agreements and other documents are usually printed in English but the small print must be read very carefully and understood otherwise you can land yourself in enormous unnecessary expenditure, even put your vessel and all within her at risk. Urea loading in the Gulf had to be carefully watched to make sure the ship would not be too deep draughted to get into the Yangtze River at the monthly tidal height of your estimated arrival time.

After our cargo of 11,000 tonnes of bagged urea had been loaded for Chittagong in the port of Umm Said, Qatar, the charter party document was presented by a white-robed official for me to sign. Right at the bottom a clause had been inserted – 'Charterers option to proceed onwards to Mongla if required'. I knew that my employers had not sent a ship to Mongla, 45 miles up the Pussur River in Bangladesh, for 20 years, though I did not know why. Our cargo was due to arrive in Chittagong only a short time before the monsoon rains came, with the result that the price of urea was rising daily as farmers became increasingly anxious to spread it on their plantations and paddy fields before the monsoon arrived. The charter party document stated that we must discharge, weather permitting, at an average rate of one thousand tonnes per day, which our hydraulic winches were perfectly capable of achieving. But with the cargo's value rising daily, the consignees tried very hard to delay us. If we got our cargo out in the 11 days allowed, it would not have achieved maximum value. If it took longer, through charterer's fault, they would have to pay us demurrage. But if the delay was caused by our ship's inefficiency, no demurrage would be incurred and we would have to pay what is called 'dispatch' money. Quite large sums were at stake. Port officials did everything possible to delay discharge, claiming daily in writing that this was my fault, demanding I sign these false statements. Which of course I did daily, but adding my own remarks about the real causes of delay. At Mongla we used an anchor chain moored to a buoy out in the river, one of a line of ships, so we were virtually at the officials' mercy. Because of my 'lack of cooperation' my wife and I were warned not to go ashore, kidnappings and worse were not uncommon.

One of these causes of delay was found to be that local persons were secretly milking hydraulic oil out of the winch lines, slowing discharge down of course, making our engineers seek to find and rectify the trouble every time. This milking of the lines could have caused a serious accident if a derrick had crashed down, as one so easily could without warning, killing somebody - an accident waiting to happen. Spurious delays were caused in numerous other ways, all blamed on me, all of which I refuted. When at last all our cargo was out and I still refused to sign 'clean sheets', a tremendous shouting match took place in my office at two in the morning, between agents, police, customs, stevedores et al - in Bangla of course but I had a good idea what they were saying. When I still refused to sign 'clean sheets' I was told to go downstream to anchor and think about it. I would be given my port clearance and have all my ship's and officers' own certificates returned when I came to see reason.

Photographed in September 1977, *Gladstone Star* once sank a light float off Brisbane. *[Fotoship/J. and M. Clarkson collection]*

Fortunately, from this anchorage downstream our Burmese Sparks managed to get a radio message to Singapore advising head office of our predicament. In another couple of days I had to ration fresh water for all onboard as a result of shoreside watchmen turning on the taps in the middle of the night, flushing precious fresh water away down the drains in the hopes that I would then have to buy 'fresh' water ashore. But Guan Guan came to the rescue by informing their Protection and Indemnity people, who sternly warned Mongla that to withold my ship illegally was tantamount to piracy. With sighs of relief I was reluctantly given all certificates plus the all-important clearance and sailed. This had indeed been an interesting lesson in shipmaster's business.

Dangerous currents

Blue Star Line's *Gladstone Star* (10,725/1957) had once run down and sunk the Breaksea Lightfloat, off the Queensland coast, when approaching Brisbane. At the time it was asked - by me also - how could you possibly hit an anchored lightfloat with its light beaming, on a fine, clear night ? Since then, however, I have learned just how suddenly and drastically one's ship can be swept off course by insidious tidal currents, almost as though guided by some malevolent giant hand. My own *Golden Grace's* brush with a large, red-painted lightfloat in the Yangtze estuary one similarly fine, dark, calm, clear night in July 1997 drove home this lesson. This large lightfloat, the *Chan Jiang Kou* (called the CJK, 'mouth of the big river'), 65 miles downriver from Shanghai, is situated to provide a roundabout which ships entering and leaving the Big River must keep to port when rounding it. While I was cautiously watching an overtaking ship closing us to starboard, and an outbound vessel coming down fine to port, the tide drove me to port sideways into the lightfloat with a resounding clang. I had underestimated

the force of the tidal flood stream, and - luckily - did not structurally damage the lightfloat - only scratched her paint, and ours amidships on the port side.

With helm hard to port to avoid catching our rudder and propeller in the lightfloat's anchor chain, we left it rocking violently in our wake with its great bell clanging (but, thank heaven, the light still flashing). Fearing dire recriminations, I reported this incident by VHF to the cruising Shanghai pilot cutter five miles ahead of us, up the fairway, to be told 'No problem Captain. We see our lightship is still afloat, still flashing correctly, bell working. Thank you for information'. *Gladstone Star*, in her brush with the Breaksea, had been less fortunate. That Australian lightfloat had sunk, at great cost to Blue Star Line.

Yes, life in Guan Guan for nine years was a great education, and for most of the time, great fun. Our Indonesians were mostly Muslims. Their country is, after all, the largest Muslim country in the world, although both Hasan and Steven were staunch Christians. Our Burmese were mostly Buddhists and we had other, to us somewhat mysterious, eastern religions onboard. But without exception each religion encouraged the others to practice their own. We were encouraged to celebrate our Christmas, the Jugoslavs their Eastern Orthodox Christmas on 6th January, while our Muslims and Buddhists celebrated numerous religious festivals, all of which demanded a party in the crew mess room for all hands not on duty. (Any excuse for a party!)

Golden Grace was sold in 1998 to a Malaysian gentleman who renamed her *Santa Suria*, offering her master and crew employment at the same rates of pay, which most gladly took. Guan Guan, realising there was now no place in modern containerised shipping for a small family company, withdrew into shoreside endeavours.

I was one of the last of the lucky ones.

THE CLIPPER FAMILY OF REEFER VESSELS
Part 1
Tony Breach

The term 'reefer' requires clarification and definition in order to fully understand the vessel type, its history, and purpose. The term is generally attributed to Knud Lauritzen during the 1930s when naming the *Pacific Reefer*, a fast refrigerated vessel with the ability to carry cargoes ranging from frozen meat to bananas and from which type today's reefer is evolved. After the Second World War the reefer could be described as a totally insulated and refrigerated cargo vessel capable of controlling temperatures between minus 18 and plus 15 degrees Centigrade as well as being able to remove field heat from tropical fruits in ambient conditions. For this purpose, adjustable, cooling air circulations to a maximum of 60 per hour were necessary, supplemented by controllable fresh air renewals up to two per hour, all being applied through deck gratings. This required a refrigeration plant of considerably greater capacity than used in refrigerated cargo liners operating in the frozen or chilled meat, fish, dairy produce and deciduous fruit trades where virtually all cargoes were loaded direct from a cold store. In addition, reefer deck heights were minimal in order to prevent product crushing and to aid the circulation of cooling air. Side ports were fitted up until the late 1980s to provide hand or conveyor loading into pre-cooled compartments. By the early1980s ships had been further developed and the optimal requirements were controlling temperatures between minus 25 or less and 15 degrees Centigrade with air circulations and fresh air supplies adjustable up to around 90 per hour and

three per hour respectively. United States Department of Agriculture equipment and certification became mandatory and most ships were also certified for the carriage of cars. Palletisation of cargoes meant the deck heights were set at 2.20 metres to correspond to contemporary truck heights.

During the 1970s the liner companies were becoming committed to containerisation and fine refrigerated cargo liners were being sold off, of which many came into the reefer trade, much of which they could handle quite well. However, occasionally one of these vessels would be fixed for a cargo for which it was unsuitable and was rejected by shippers. The reefer operators then coined the term 'pure reefer' for their ships to differentiate between the two types, but this term has lapsed as all of the old liners have now disappeared. In the 21st century the reefer is becoming more sophisticated in its cargo handling, and grating-less decks are being introduced together with deck heights increased to around 2.65 metres in order to compete with the high-cube integrated reefer container. It seems certain that most future new buildings will be of the side-loading type.

Within the reefer sector cost calculations are invariably referred to in United States' currency per cubic foot of refrigerated space. Thus charter rates and earnings are expressed in US cents/cubic foot/30 days while new-building costs are expressed in US dollars per cubic foot. This notwithstanding that some recent fixtures have been made in US dollars/square metre of refrigerated deck area and that some other currencies may be applied.

Pacific Reefer of 1935 introduced the term 'reefer'. She became *African Reefer* in 1936, and is seen here at Vancouver on 26th January 1963, shortly before she was sold to breakers in the Netherlands. *[F.W. Hawks]*

First of the class, *Golar Nel*, as owned by Trygve Gotaas A/S of Tvedestrand and in Salen colours. *[J. and M. Clarkson]*

The shipbuilders and their ships

In November 1967 a reefer was launched at Drammen which was to be the first of a family of 40 vessels in three groups which evolved over a period of nine years and were built over a period of 14 years. The first ship, *Golar Nel* of 310,000 cubic feet insulated space, was built for Trygve Gotaas of Norway for Liberian flag operation by the Gotaas-Larsen organisation and had one sister vessel built at Horten for the same group. This group of ships later became known as 'Pre-Clippers'.

The third ship was the *Golar Frost* in 1968 which was basically identical to the first two ships but with the addition of a forecastle which increased the capacity to 340,500 cubic feet of insulated space. Twelve of these vessels were built at Drammen with three going to Gotaas-Larsen and two being launched for other Norwegian owners, one of which was sold on the stocks to nominees of Maritime Fruit Carriers. A further seven were built for Maritime Fruit Carriers' nominees, five under the flag of the Federal Republic of Germany and two under the British flag.

Golar Frost again in Salen colours. *[FotoFlite incorporating Skyfotos, 282477]*

A further eight vessels were built at Middlesbrough for operation by Maritime Fruit Carriers' nominees under the British flag. They were all named after major British ports with the second word of the name being *Clipper*; hence the family name of the ships. Two vessels were also built at Sandefjord for DSR Reefers of the German Democratic Republic.

All 22 of these ships were referred to as 'Standard Clippers' and until 1975 were continually evolving as construction progressed. In particular there was an increase of insulated space to 354,000 cubic feet attained by careful adjustment of the fitting of the insulation and hold linings. However, the final Drammen ship and the two Horten ships are shown by all sources to be of more than 362,000 cubic feet which may result from the fitting to these three of a smaller, eight-cylinder engine, and for these reasons they may be considered as transitional to the 'Super Clippers'. The original engines were of the Sulzer nine-cylinder RD type rated at 12,000 BHP but these were superceded in 1972 by the nine-cylinder RND type rated at 14,850 BHP and in the three final ships by the eight-cylinder RND type rated at 13,200 BHP. Power generation capacity was also increased and later vessels were outfitted with four auxiliary engines instead of the three of the earlier ships.

The final development within the family was the 'Super Clipper' which was lengthened by a little less than five metres resulting in an increase of insulated space to 381,500 cubic feet, which increased to 398,000 cubic feet in later vessels. The first vessel was built at Drammen in 1973 as the *Wild Flamingo* for the Federal Steam Navigation Co. Ltd. who also took three others of the group. Two Drammen vessels went to the Portuguese TRANSFRUTA group, and three were built for COMANAV of Morocco. Two went to Peter Y. Berg of the family that owned the Drammen shipyard together with one built at Haugesund, and Flota Bananera of Ecuador took the final three built at Drammen plus one built at Tonsberg.

The evolution of the 'Super Clippers', apart from the increase in size, included a further engine change from the Sulzer eight-cylinder RND type to the six-cylinder RND rated at 11,400 BHP. Ship owners also requested some modifications to suit their own operations including different cargo gear for the second two Federal ships and one of the Berg ships and the fitting of twin hatches at holds 2 and 3 in the final COMANAV vessel.

In service
The 'Clippers' were a very successful design for both builders and owners. The introduction of the class coincided with the containerisation of many of the refrigerated liner services and the expansion of production and consumption of perishable foodstuffs, particularly fruit. While the container is an excellent medium for immediate post-harvest storage, transportation and just-in-time delivery, it cannot cope with moving large seasonal harvests of fruit from the southern hemisphere's producers to the industrial nations in the northern hemisphere.

The emergence of Maritime Fruit Carriers of Haifa as a major owner of reefer shipping together with Salen Reefer Services of Stockholm, who operated them in a pooling arrangement, was significant as it allowed for the efficient employment of reefers within a vast trading network. The subsequent financial failure of Maritime Fruit Carriers in 1976 resulted in the sale of all their vessels to various owners world-wide. Some companies, particularly British, who had previously operated refrigerated liner tonnage acquired Maritime Fruit Carriers vessels including 'Clippers'. Cunard placed their acquired 'Clippers' and other reefers into the Salen Reefers pool while Blue Star were still operating refrigerated liner services as well as expanding their reefer operations and had sufficient experience for the two 'Clippers' they bought. P&O ordered four 'Super Clippers' from the Drammen yard for their Federal subsidiary and entered into a joint venture with J. Lauritzen as Lauritzen Peninsular

Wild Flamingo wearing P&O funnel colours. *[World Ship Society Ltd.]*

Reefers. As an indication of the importance of the 'Clippers' within the reefer shipping community it is interesting to note that a normal barometer for the trade was the current 'Clipper' charter rate and for the sale and purchase business the current US dollar value of a 'Clipper' after adjustment for age.

There is no doubt that the 'Clippers' had some shortcomings which were possibly attributable to the design being something of a quart in a pint pot at a reasonable price. Stability was a problem in most reefers of the period due to the very high fuel consumption in a relatively small vessel with a very fine hull. The addition of a large forecastle in the 'Standard' and 'Super Clippers' and the consequent increase of cargo volume above the original centres of gravity further reduced the stability and in order to deal with this all double bottom and wing heavy fuel oil tanks in the 'Standards' were also suitable for water ballast. In the case of the 'Supers' there was better subdivision of tanks and there was a slightly reduced water ballast capacity. The 'Standards' built for Maritime Fruit Carriers were also equipped to allow heavy fuel oil to be carried in the forepeak tanks which were extremely susceptible to spilling. The vessels were reasonably well equipped with good quality machinery and reefer plant plus the latest in navigational aids.

A major shortcoming in all reefers at the time was that they were unprepared for the revolution in palletised cargo handling and it had not yet been learned that road haulage vehicles would set the pallet stack height at around 2.10 metres. The result was a requirement for a minimum deck height in reefer vessels of 2.20 metres in order to allow for good cooling air circulation. The 'Clippers' had lower deck heights but were well designed for break-bulk fruit handling in having five shell doors on each side and were also capable of operating with conveyors or pocket elevators through partially opened main and 'tween deck hatch covers. Nevertheless, some cargoes were supplied on reduced-height pallets although the five-ton cargo gear, which was quite normal for reefers of the period, was considered to be a little light for pallet handling. Likewise the cargo gratings were of insufficient strength to handle fork lift trucks and suffered much damage. Accommodation was rather cramped but to the normal standard of a fairly small ship for the period and it was fully air-conditioned.

Pre-Clippers

Fleet list entries are in the usual Ships in Focus style. Unless stated otherwise, the flag of the vessel is that of the owning company, the first name in an ownership entry. Names of beneficial owners, where known, are given in brackets before those of the managers.

Built by Drammen Slip and Verksted, Drammen, Norway.

Yard No. 63 **GOLAR NEL**
IMO 6805464 4,902g 2,435n 7,095d
139.27 x 130.61 x 18.01 x 11.64 metres
Refrigerated capacity: 310,357 cubic feet
9-cyl. 2SCSA 9RD68-type oil engine by Sulzer Brothers Ltd., Winterthur, Switzerland; 12,000 BHP, 22.5 knots.
3.11.1967: Launched for Trygve Gotaas A/S, Tvedestrand (Gotaas-Larsen Inc, New York, USA) as GOLAR NEL.
1968: Completed.
1975: Sold to Zapryba', Kaliningrad, USSR and renamed BRESTSKAYA KREPOST.
Prior to 1983: Transferred to Mortransflot, Kaliningrad, USSR.
1990: Sold to Vivarini Compania Naviera S.A., Panama (Pan Group S.A., Piraeus, Greece) and renamed S. LUCIA under the Honduras flag.
Prior to 10.11.1992: Laid up at Istanbul.
21.10.1993: Arrived at Aliaga in tow from Istanbul for demolition by Ogi Gemi Sokum Ticaret A.S.

Golar Nel as *Brestskaya Krepost*, registered in Kaliningrad following sale to the USSR in 1975. *[Michael D.J. Lennon]*

Built by Marinens Hovedverft, Horten, Norway.

Yard No. 164 **GOLAR FREEZE**
IMO 6828741 6,709g 3,755n 7,095d
139.36 x 130.61 x 18.00 x 11.64 metres
Refrigerated capacity: 310,357 cubic feet
9-cyl. 2SCSA 9RD68-type oil engine
by Marinens Hovedverft, Horten;
12,000 BHP, 22.5 knots.
19.4.1968: Launched for Golarfreeze
Inc., Monrovia, Liberia (Gotaas-Larsen
Inc., New York, USA, managers) as
GOLAR FREEZE.
3.10.1968: Completed.
1976: Transferred to Intercontinental
Transportation Services Ltd., Monrovia
(Standard Fruit and Steamship Co.,
New Orleans, USA) (Gotaas-Larsen
Inc., New York, USA, managers) and
renamed LIMON.
1978: Managers became Irgens Larsen
A/S, Oslo, Norway, and beneficial
owners Castle and Cooke Inc.,
Honolulu, USA.
1984: Transferred to Mahele Reefer
Ltd., Monrovia (Standard Fruit and
Steamship Co., New Orleans, USA)
(Irgens Larsen A/S, Oslo, managers)
1992: Beneficial owners became Dole
Fresh Fruit International Ltd., San Jose,
Costa Rica.
20.6.1993: Arrived at Alang for
demolition.
15.7.1993: Work commenced by
Lalchand Rani and Sons.

Golar Freeze. [FotoFlite incorporating Skyfotos, 282478]

STANDARD CLIPPERS

Built by Drammen Slip and Verksted, Drammen, Norway.

Yard No.64. **GOLAR FROST**
IMO 6831602 7,173g 4,115n 7,400d
139.27 x 130.00 x 18.01 x 11.64 metres
Refrigerated capacity: 340,477 cubic
feet
9-cyl. 2SCSA 9RD68-type oil engine
by Sulzer Brothers Ltd., Winterthur,
Switzerland; 12,000 BHP, 22.5 knots.
25.5.1968: Launched for Golarfrost
Inc., Monrovia, Liberia (Gotaas-Larsen
Inc., New York, USA, managers) as
GOLAR FROST.
1968: Completed.

1976: Transferred to Intercontinental
Transportation Services Ltd. (Standard
Fruit and Steamship Co., New Orleans,
USA), Monrovia (Irgens Larsen
A/S, Oslo, managers) and renamed
BOLIVAR.
1985: Transferred to Compania Naviera
Agmaresa S.A., Guayaquil, Ecuador
(Standard Fruit and Steamship Co.,
New Orleans, USA) (Irgens Larsen
A/S, Oslo, managers) and renamed RIO
DAULE.
1992: Beneficial owners became Dole
Fresh Fruit International Ltd., San Jose,
Costa Rica.
1993: Transferred to Liberian flag.
28.5.1998: Arrived Alang for
demolition.

Golar Frost as *Bolivar.* Note the Dole logo on the side of her bridge. *[Tony Breach collection]*

Slevik as Alaska. [World Ship Society Ltd.]

Yard No.65. **SLEVIK**
IMO 6905290 6,704/4889g
3,544/2439n 9,186d
140.72 x 131.93 x 18.00 x 11.64 metres
Refrigerated capacity: 347,049 cubic feet
9-cyl. 2SCSA 9RD68-type oil engine
by Sulzer Brothers Ltd., Winterthur,
Switzerland; 12,000 BHP, 22.5 knots.
19.12.1968: Launched for Karlander
Reefer A/S, Fredrikstad, Norway as
SLEVIK.
1969: Completed for Intermare K.G.,
K.S. Kuhlschiffe G.m.b.H. and Co.,
Munich and later Hamburg, West
Germany (Maritime Fruit Carriers
Co. Ltd., Haifa, Israel) (Christian F.
Ahrenkiel, Hamburg, managers) as

ALASKACORE.
1975: Renamed ALASKA.
1979: Renamed ALASKA 1.
1980: Transferred to Panama flag.
1984: Renamed ALASKA.
1986: Sold to Panavista Maritime Inc.
(Fotis C. Georgopoulos, Piraeus) (Akra
Shipping Co. Ltd., Piraeus, Greece,
managers) and renamed NISSOS
SKOPELOS.
13.11.1986: Developed a list after
taking on water during heavy weather
east of the Azores while on a voyage
from Amsterdam to Cuba with a cargo
of potatoes.
15.11.1986: Sank in position 39.42
north, 21.24 west. No lives were lost.

Yard No.66. **GOLAR BORG**
IMO 7002291 4,892g 2,435n 7,475d
140.70 x 131.93 x 18.00 x 11.64 meters
Refrigerated capacity: 349,790 cubic feet
9-cyl. 2SCSA 9RD68-type oil engine
by Sulzer Brothers Ltd., Winterthur,
Switzerland; 12,000 BHP, 22.5 knots.
7.7.1969: Launched for I/S Golar Borg
(Irgens Larsen A/S, managers), Oslo,
Norway as GOLAR BORG.
12.1969: Completed for Trygve Gotaas
A/S (Irgens Larsen A/S, managers),
Oslo
31.10.1978: Abandoned west of the
Azores in position 38.15 north by 40.10
west after developing a heavy list when
her cargo shifted in heavy weather

Golar Borg. [FotoFlite incorporating Skyfotos, 258638]

during a voyage from Rostock to Havana with a cargo of potatoes. Four crew members were lost.

Yard No.67. ANTARCTICORE
IMO 7006297 6,699/4,889g
3,662/2,438n 7,578d
140.72 x 131.93 x 18.00 x 11.64 metres
Refrigerated capacity: 347,049 cubic feet
9-cyl. 2SCSA 9RND68-type oil engine by Sulzer Brothers Ltd., Winterthur, Switzerland; 12,000 BHP, 22.5 knots.
18.12.1969: Launched for Intermare K.G., K.S. Kuhlschiffe G.m.b.H. and Co., Munich and later Hamburg, West Germany (Maritime Fruit Carriers Co. Ltd., Haifa, Israel) (Christian F. Ahrenkiel, Hamburg, managers) as ANTARCTICORE.
30. 4.1970: Completed.
1975: Renamed ANTARCTIC.
1980: Registered in Panama.
1984: Registered in West Germany.
1986: Sold to Richmede Holdings Inc., Monrovia, Liberia (Akra Shipping Co. Ltd. (Fotis C. Georgopoulos), Piraeus, Greece) and renamed NISSOS SKIATHOS under the Greek flag.
1988: Transferred to Reefskyth Shipping Co. Ltd., Panama (Akra Shipping Co. Ltd., Piraeus, Greece (Fotis C. Georgopoulos), Piraeus, Greece) under the Greek flag.
1988: Sold to Magna Compania Naviera S.A., Panama (Transcontinental Maritime and Trading S.A. (Comninos Brothers), Piraeus) and renamed SKIATHOS REEFER.
1992: Sold to Magna Compania Naviera S.A. (Castle Shipholdings S.A., Piraeus).
11.6.1992: Laid up at Eleusis.
7.7.1993: Sank in Nantong River, Shanghai, following collision with the Chinese motor vessel TIAN MU SHAN (IMO 7525401, 9,318/78) during voyage to breakers. Presumed salvaged and demolished.

Yard No.68. BERINGCORE
IMO 7024108 6,682/4,899g
3,623/2,438n 9,109/7,689d
140.72 x 130.00 x 18.00 x 11.64 metres
Refrigerated capacity: 346,541 cubic feet
9-cyl. 2SCSA 9RND68-type oil engine by Sulzer Brothers Ltd., Winterthur, Switzerland; 14,850 BHP, 23.25 knots.
1.7.1970: Launched for F.M. Atlantic Frigomaris Kuhlschiffreederei G.m.b.H. and Co. K.G., Hamburg, West Germany (Maritime Fruit Carriers Co. Ltd., Haifa, Israel) as BERINGCORE.
10.9.1970: Completed.
1975: Renamed BERING.

Antarcticore on 8th August 1973. *[J. and M. Clarkson collection]*

Skiathos Reefer, the former *Antarcticore*, wearing Lauritzen's funnel colours but under the Greek flag and ownership. The photograph was taken between 1988 and her loss in 1993. *[Michael D.J. Lennon]*

1975: Sold to Bonita Ocean Steam Ship Co., Monrovia, Liberia (Noboa Group, Guayaquil, Ecuador) (Gotaas-Larsen Inc., New York, USA) and renamed BONITA.
1979: Transferred to Naviera Del Pacifico S.A. (Noboa Group), Guayaquil (A/S Irgens Larsen, Oslo, Norway).
14.12.1981: Sank in the English Channel in position 50.05 north, 02.13 west after developing a severe list in storm force conditions during a voyage from Hamburg to Puerto Limon with a cargo of fertiliser. One crew member was lost but 36 survivors including some women and children were rescued from the ship's lifeboats by helicopters and the St. Peter Port lifeboat.

Beringcore, *[J. and M. Clarkson collection]*

Yard No.69 **GREENLANDCORE**
IMO 7038800 6,682/4,876g
3,623/2,514n 9,109/7,689d
140.70 x 130.00 x 18.00 x 11.64 metres
Refrigerated capacity: 346,183 cubic feet
9-cyl. 2SCSA 9RND68-type oil engine
by Sulzer Brothers Ltd., Winterthur,
Switzerland; 14,850 BHP, 23.25 knots.
30.11.1970: Launched for F.M.
Baltic Frigomaris Kuhlschiffe
Reederei G.m.b.H. & Co., Hamburg,
West Germany (Maritime Fruit
Carriers Co. Ltd., Haifa, Israel) as
GREENLANDCORE.
2.1971: Completed as GREENLAND.
1975: Sold to Spanocean Line Ltd.
(Salen U.K. Ltd.), London and renamed
CAYMAN.
1976: Sold to Société de Navigation
Maghrebine, Casablanca, Morocco
(Salen U.K. Ltd., London) and renamed
SMARA.
1976: Transferred to Union Maritime
Marocco-Scandinavie 'UNIMAR',
Casablanca (Salen U.K. Ship
Management Ltd., London).
1987: Sold to Western Continent S.A.,
Panama (Transcontinental Maritime and
Trading S.A.) (Comninos Brothers),
Piraeus, Greece and renamed ITHAKA
REEFER.
1991: Transferred to Blaze Navigation
S.A., Panama (Transcontinental
Maritime and Trading S.A. (Comninos
Brothers), Piraeus) and renamed
PACIFIC TRADER.
1992: Managers became Target Marine
S.A. (Anthony E. Comninos), Piraeus.
24. 5.1994: Arrived at Alang for
demolition.

Yard No.70 **ICELAND**
IMO 7107792 6,670/4,870g
3,624/2,515n 9,109/7,689d
140.70 x 130.00 x 18.00 x 11.64 metres
Refrigerated capacity: 353,392 cubic feet
9-cyl. 2SCSA 9RND68-type oil engine
by Sulzer Brothers Ltd., Winterthur,
Switzerland; 14,850 BHP, 23.25 knots.
4.1971: Launched for F.M. Caribic
Frigomaris Kuhlschiffe Reederei
G.m.b.H. & Co., Hamburg (Maritime
Fruit Carriers Co. Ltd., Haifa, Israel) as
ICELAND.
17.7.1971: Completed.
1978: Transferred to Reefer Caribic
Ganymed Schiffahrtgesellschaft m.b.H.,
Hamburg.
1979: Transferred to Cape Wrath
Shipping Co., Panama (Reefer Pacific
Ganymed Schiffahrtgesellschaft m.b.H.,
Hamburg).
1984: Sold to Hertel Shipping S.A.,

Greenland on 10th July 1971. *[J. and M. Clarkson collection]*

Smara of Union Maritime Marocco-Scandinavie 'UNIMAR', Casablanca was
completed as *Greenlandcore*. *[Tony Breach collection]*

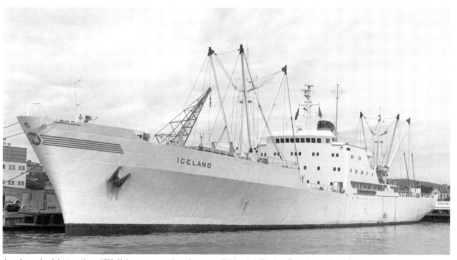

Iceland. Note the 'FM' logo on the bow. *[World Ship Society Ltd.]*

Panama (Trans Pacific Transport System
Inc., Manila, Philippines) and renamed
ATITLAN under the Philippines flag.
1985: Sold to Rosemary Maritime
Corporation, Panama (Ganymed
Schiffahrtgesellschaft m.b.H.,
Hamburg) and renamed ICELAND.
1985: Sold to Transportes Frigorificos
Uruguayo S.A. 'Transfusa',
Montevideo, Uruguay and renamed
URUCITRUS.

1988: Sold to Reefna Shipping Ltd.,
Floriana, Malta (Fotis C. Georgopoulos
Shipping Co., Piraeus, Greece) and
renamed NISSOS NAXOS.
1988: Transferred to Cricket Shipping
Co. Ltd. (Transcontinental Maritime
and Trading S.A. (Comninos Brothers),
Piraeus, Greece and renamed NAXOS
REEFER.
1991: Transferred to Benefit Maritime
S.A. (Transcontinental Maritime and

Iceland in Salen funnel colours. *[Michael D.J. Lennon]*

Iceland as *Unicitrus*, owned in Uruguay. *[Russell Priest]*

Trading S.A. (Comninos Brothers)), Piraeus and renamed ATLANTIC TRADER

1991: Transferred to Target Marine S.A. (Anthony E. Comninos), Piraeus.

15.7.1993: Arrived Ningbo for demolition.

Yard No.71 **NORDLAND**
IMO 7120809 6,677/4,870g
3,637/2,529n 9,144d
140.70 x 130.00 x 18.00 x 11.64 metres
Refrigerated capacity: 353,992 cubic feet
9-cyl. 2SCSA 9RND68-type oil engine
by Sulzer Brothers Ltd., Winterthur,
Switzerland; 14,850 BHP, 23.25 knots.

16.7.1971: Launched for Frigomaris Kuhlschiffe Reederei G.m.b.H. & Co., Hamburg, West Germany (Maritime Fruit Carriers Co. Ltd., Haifa, Israel) as NORDLAND.

8.12.1971: Completed.

1977: Transferred to Reefer Pacific Ganymed Schiffahrtges m.b.H., Hamburg (Maritime Fruit Carriers Co. Ltd., Haifa).

1979: Renamed NORDLAND V under the Panama flag.

1984: Sold to Hertel Shipping S.A., Panama (Trans Pacific Transport System Inc., Manila, Philippines) and renamed ARAWAK under the Philippines flag.

1985: Sold to Alis Shipping Co. S.A., Panama (Ganymed

Nordland. [FotoFlite incorporating Skyfotos, 257977]

Schiffahrtgesellschaft m.b.H., Hamburg) and renamed NORDLAND V.

1987: Sold to Enos Compania Naviera S.A., Panama (Akra Shipping Co. Ltd. (Fotis C. Georgopoulos Shipping Co.), Piraeus, Greece) and renamed NISSOS PAROS under the Greek flag.

1990: Sold to Balance Reefer Services Ltd., Douglas, Isle of Man (Seascot Shiptrading Ltd., Glasgow) and renamed ARCTIC C.

1990: Sold to Stockport Shipping Co. Ltd., Limassol, Cyprus (International Reefer Services S.A. (Costas Comninos), Piraeus) and renamed ARCTIC REEFER.

1992: Transferred to Marine Champion S.A., Panama (International Reefer Services S.A. (Costas Comninos), Piraeus).

1.1.1994: Sank about 160 miles off Miyazaki in position 29.23 north, 133.26 east after her hull fractured during a voyage from Tiannjin, China to Venezuela with a cargo of 4,222 tons of bagged beans. Seventeen crew members were lost. The loss was partly attributed to inadequate repairs to damage caused by collision with the Panama-flag motor vessel STELLA FAIRY (IMO 8403325, 3,150/1984) on 5.4.1993 at Yokohama as a result of dragging an anchor.

Nordland as *Arctic C. [Ian J. Farquhar]*

The final name of *Nordland* was *Arctic Reefer*, carried under Comninos ownership from 1990 until her loss in 1994. *[Michael D.J. Lennon]*

Lapland. [FotoFlite incorporating Skyfotos, 347297]

Yard No.72 **LAPLAND**
IMO 7203663 6,671/4,905g
3,641/2,618n 8,950d
140.62 x 131.88 x 18.01 x 11.64m
Refrigerated capacity: 353,992 cubic
feet.
9-cyl. 2SCSA 9RND68-type oil engine
by Sulzer Brothers Ltd., Winterthur,
Switzerland; 14,850 BHP, 23.25 knots.
14.1.1972: Launched for Elsden
Shipping Lines Ltd. (Maritime Fruit
Carriers Co. Ltd., Haifa, Israel)
(Whitco Marine Services Ltd.,
London).

4.1972: Completed as LAPLAND.
1976: Transferred to Mentary Ltd.,
Glasgow (Salen U.K. Shipmanagement
Ltd., London) and renamed
KUNGSHAMN.
1978: Sold to Union Maritime
Marocco-Scandinavie, UNIMAR,
Casablanca, Morocco (Salen U.K.
Shipmanagement Ltd., London) and
renamed SIJILMASSA.
1990: Sold to Lucida Maritime S.A.
(Transcontinental Maritime and
Trading (Comninos Brothers), Piraeus,
Greece) and renamed BOLIVAR

TRADER under the Bahamas flag.
1991: Transferred to Target Marine
S.A. (Anthony E. Comninos), Piraeus.
1994: Sold to Richard Fares
Enterprises Pty. Ltd., Fremantle,
Australia and renamed FARID F under
the St Vincent flag.
1996: Converted to a livestock carrier.
2006: Sold to Torrens Investments
(Private) Ltd., Singapore (Inco Ships
Pty. Ltd., Sydney, New South Wales)
and renamed TORRENS under the flag
of Tonga.
17.8.2010: Still in service.

Left: *Lapland* as the Moroc-
can *Sijilmassa*. [*J. and M.
Clarkson*]

Below: In 1996 the former
Lapland was converted to a
livestock carrier to move live
sheep from Australia to the
Middle East. She is seen as
Torrens, a name she took
in 2006, on 4th April 2008.
Note the array of ventilators.
[*Ron Mew, Mt. Maunganui*]

Labrador Clipper. [Russell Priest]

Yard No.73 **LABRADOR CLIPPER**
IMO 7217559 6,671/4,905g
3,641/2,618n 9,168/7,772d
140.70 x 131.25 x 18.00 x 11.64 metres
Refrigerated capacity: 353,544 cubic feet
9-cyl. 2SCSA 9RND68-type oil engine
by Sulzer Brothers Ltd., Winterthur,
Switzerland; 14,850 BHP, 23.25 knots.
24.5.1972: Launched for Chichester

Shipping Lines Ltd., Glasgow
(Maritime Fruit Carriers Co. Ltd.,
Haifa, Israel) as LABRADOR
CLIPPER
1972: Completed.
1976: Sold to Blue Star Line Ltd. (Blue
Star Ship Management Ltd.), London
and renamed TUSCAN STAR.
1980: Sold to Sun Glory Compania

Naviera S.A., Panama (Diana Shipping
Agencies S.A. (S.P. Palios), Piraeus,
Greece) and renamed CHIOS PRIDE
under the Greek flag.
1993: Sold to Galla Compania Naviera
S.A. (Aquila Shipping and Investment
Co. S.A.), Piraeus.
27.3.1993: Arrived at Mumbai for
demolition.

The former *Labrador Clipper* was in Blue Star ownership between 1976 and 1980 as *Tuscan Star*. She retained her original
Glasgow registration. *[FotoFlite incorporating Skyfotos/J. and M. Clarkson collection]*

Golar Ragni with a bone between her teeth. The Clippers were credited with a speed of 23 knots. *[Tony Breach collection]*

Yard No.74 **KONGSFJELL**
IMO 7230173 6,671/4,905g
3,641/2,618n 9,218/7,722d
140.62 x 131.88 x 18.01 x 11.64 metres
Refrigerated capacity: 353,544 cubic feet
9-cyl. 2SCSA 9RND68-type oil engine
by Sulzer Brothers Ltd., Winterthur,
Switzerland; 14,850 BHP, 23.25 knots.

6.10.1972: Launched for Norwegian
owners as KONGSFJELL.
12.1972: Completed for Trygve Gotaas
A/S, Tvedestrand, Norway (Gotaas
Larsen A/S, Oslo) as GOLAR RAGNI.
1976: Sold to Peter Y. Berg, Drammen,
Norway and renamed RAGNI BERG.
1977: Sold to Corporacion Venezolan

di Fumento S.A., Caracas, Venezuela
and renamed SIERRA NEVADA.
1986: Renamed PUERTO CABELLO.
1987: with last entry as SIERRA
NEVADA.
5.1998: Reported scrapped. She had
been deleted from 'Lloyd's Register' in
1987.

Ragni Berg. [Ian J. Farquhar]

Yard No.75 **GOLAR GIRL**
IMO 7305760 6,682/4,829g
3,605/2,459n 9,218/7,722d
140.62 x 131.88 x 18.01 x 11.64 metres
Refrigerated capacity: 363,047 cubic feet
8-cyl. 2SCSA 8RND68 oil engine by A/S Horten Verft, Horten; 13,200 BHP, 23 knots.
8.2.1973: Launched for I/S Golar Girl (Irgens Larsen A/S), Oslo, Norway as GOLAR GIRL.
5.1973: Completed.
1977: Transferred to I/S Hilco Girl, Tvedestrand, Norway (Irgens Larsen

A/S, Oslo), and renamed HILCO GIRL.
1981: Sold to Eastern Reefers (Private) Ltd., Singapore. (Thome & Co. (Private) Ltd.) and renamed TIMUR GIRL.
1983: Sold to Silver Sand Shipping S.A., Monrovia, Liberia (Enterprises Shipping and Trading S.A., Piraeus, Greece) and renamed LUCKY under the Greek flag.
1984: Name amended to LUCKY 1.
1984: Sold to Naviera Del Pacifico S.A. 'NAPACA' (Noboa Group), Guayaquil, Ecuador (Irgens Larsen A/S, Oslo) and renamed CIUDAD DE GUAYAQUIL.

1988: Renamed PROVINCIA DEL GUAYAS.
1990: Managers became Ecuadorian Line N.V., Guayaquil
1995: Transferred to Conception Island Shipping Ltd., Nassau, Bahamas (Noboa Group) (Ecuadorian Line N.V., Guayaquil) and renamed BALTIC SEA.
1997: Managers became Trireme Vessels Management N.V., Antwerp.
11.2009: Reported sold to Peruvian breakers.

To be continued.

Above: *Golar Girl.* [FotoFlite incorporating Skyfotos, 282475]

Left: *Golar Girl* under the Ecuador flag as *Provincia del Guayas.* [Russell Priest]

THE FIRST MISTLEY

Gerry Lewis

Two views of Horlock's *Mistley* grounded in the River Welland on 20th March 1908. Who at the time would have imagined that this tiny steamer would be earning her living half a century later? *[Michael Elsden collection]*

Mistley in an unidentified port on 29th March 1928. *[J. and M. Clarkson collection]*

I was most interested to read 'A Tale of Two *Mistleys*' in 'Record' 44. I appreciate that the article was concerned with ships named *Mistley* which were in the ownership of W.N. Lindsay Ltd., the first being purchased from F.W. Horlock's Ocean Transport Co. Ltd. of Harwich. However, there was an earlier vessel named *Mistley* built for the Horlock family in 1906.

In 1908 *Mistley* made a voyage into the River Welland to the town of Spalding, about 12 miles inland from the Wash, with a cargo of 120 tons of manure. The Welland is narrow and at that time was tidal through the town, with high grass banks on either side. On 20th March 1908 the *Mistley* grounded about one mile short of her destination. As the tide ebbed, the current rushed with great force either side of the *Mistley* and undermined the banks, a portion of which were carried away. To assist in refloating her on the next tide, 26 tons of manure were unloaded by hand. The following day she reached the head of navigation by the town's High Bridge, discharging her cargo to a local yard.

Mistley was by far the largest vessel to navigate the Welland as far as the town centre, but barges owned by B. W. Steamship, Tug and Lighter Co. Ltd. of Hull were towed up the river to within half a mile of the High Bridge to serve mills owned by G.F. Birch, a partner in the B. W. company. Until the late 1950s coastal steamers including *G.F.B.*, *Gwendolynne Birch*, *Buoyant* and the motor vessel *Fosdyke Trader* (ex-*Empire Fathom*) traded up the Welland as far as Fosdyke Wharf, about eight miles downstream of Spalding.

Two photographs in my possession show *Mistley* on her one and only voyage to Spalding. They feature in two books on Spalding, the authors of which found dates and details of her voyage in local newspapers for March 1908. The vessel beyond *Mistley* in the stern view is a billy boy, a type of sailing coaster many of which were owned in Spalding. They traded mainly along the East Coast and brought coal to Spalding Gas Works, situated about a quarter of a mile further upstream.

In the early 1950s a new, three-mile waterway, the Coronation Channel, was built around the town to prevent the flooding which occurred in

1947. Tidal sluice gates were provided where the water from the Coronation Channel re-entered the Welland on the seaward side of the town. Lock gates were built in the river just upstream of the sluice gates so that the Welland through the town is no longer tidal, and it remains an attractive feature of the town.

MISTLEY (1) 1906-1919

O.N. 123931 135g 59n
85.0 x 19.5 x 7.6 feet
1911: 153g 82n
103.0 x 19.5 x 7.6 feet
C. 2-cyl. (23 and 11 x 15 inches) by Crabtree and Co. Ltd., Yarmouth; 28 NHP, 150 IHP, 7 knots.
1906: Completed by Crabtree and Co. Ltd., Yarmouth for Frederick W. Horlock, Mistley as MISTLEY.
1911: Lengthened.
1919: Sold to Joseph T. and Bertram J. Leete, London and renamed CATHERINE ETHEL.
14.7.1922: Transferred to J.T. Leete and Sons Ltd., London.
2.3.1923: Sold to William H. Müller and Co. (London) Ltd., London.
20.5.1924: Transferred to the Vianda

The *Catherine Ethel* photographed in the early 1950s. Although she has been fitted out as a sand dredger she still has her cargo derrick. *[J. and M. Clarkson collection]*

Steamship Co. Ltd. (William H. Müller and Co. (London) Ltd., manager), London.
29.4.1939: Sold to Hugh Hamlin, George J. Hamlin and George W. Fairney, Cardiff and converted to a suction dredger during the 1940s.
11.1.1963: Sold to Metal Trading (Swansea) Ltd., Swansea.

15.1.1963: Sold to Thomas L. Jones, Swansea*.
13.6.1973: Register closed, broken up. She may have been demolished as early as 1969.
* 'Lloyd's Register' gives owners as Llanelly Quarries Ltd. (T.L. Jones, manager), Swansea. The registered owner was Jones, the manager of the quarry.

RECORD REVIEWS

There are interesting challenges to researching and publishing shipbuilding histories. Successful yards have tended to produce more vessels than all but the largest shipping companies owned. Hence, fully detailing a builders' output – even when the ships' histories can all be traced – is a major task when a yard lists may easily have 500 to 1,000 entries. Because yards changed hands and names from time to time, shipbuilding is often treated on a regional basis, with all the builders in a port or a particular region being chronicled. This allows geographical factors such as access to deep water, to customers, materials and a workforce to be considered in depth, but brings in a major additional difficulty in tracing the historical (or even pre-historical) origins of shipbuilding in a given area, let alone cataloguing all the ships built there.

Despite the difficulties, shipbuilding historians may well have richer seams to mine than those who research ship owners. The builder has to display mastery of technology, and – if he is to prosper – to stay abreast or preferably ahead of technical developments. Indeed, the builder will often have an influence on ship design, construction and performance that few ship owners can claim. With expensive plant and a core of skilled employees, the builder must also weather the inevitable downturns in trade cycles. Financial management of an operation that, especially in hard times, often involves providing finance to prospective customers, is also a key factor in understanding the history of a builder, although one that is discussed far too infrequently. The complexity of labour relations in shipbuilding is another topic often ignored in formal histories of shipbuilders, although there is much academic interest in this field, largely seeking to dispel the widely held view that trade unions were solely to blame for the demise of British shipbuilding.

Probably because they are more difficult to produce well, good histories of shipbuilders are rarer than those of shipping companies, so the two volumes reviewed here, although very different in format, are both welcome.

LIFFEY SHIPS AND SHIPBUILDING
Pat Sweeney
13.5 x 21.5cms softback of 320 pages
Published by Mercier Press, Cork, 2010 at £19.50

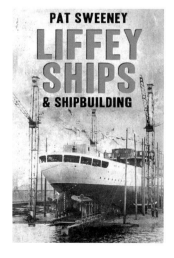

Iron and steel shipbuilding in Ireland's major city and port has had a chequered history, with a number of builders arriving, more-or-less flourishing, and then disappearing. The first builders to be well documented were Walpole and Webb, established by 1863 and soon to become Walpole, Webb and Bewley. They built both their first steamship and their first screw steamer in 1865, but were in financial difficulties by 1870 after delivering over 50 vessels, mostly small.

Following this failure, Dublin's shipping fraternity turned envious eyes on Belfast, where shipbuilding was going from strength to strength under Edward Harland and Gustav Wolff. It was argued that the numerous ship owners based in Dublin not only needed local repair facilities, but were also potential customers for new buildings. Early in the twentieth century two Scottish shipbuilders were persuaded to set up the

Dublin Dockyard Company, which enjoyed modest success until a combination of a shipping recession, steel shortages and poor labour relations forced its closure in 1922. Vickers Ltd. then bought the yard as a going concern, and struggled for 15 years to make it pay, building about 50 ships ranging from lighters for the Grand Canal to substantial seagoing cargo ships, and repairing many more. The yard re-opened again as the Liffey Dockyard Ltd. in October 1940 to carry out much-needed repairs to neutral Ireland's depleted merchant fleet, and help reconstruct some of the wrecks the country was forced to buy to meet its shipping needs. Some repair work was done on British vessels trading to Ireland, with the UK supplying the steel, and – surprisingly – there was considerable discussion in London about the UK ordering ships from the yard. During post-war years the yard continued mainly with repair work, but also launched a few ships for local ship owners or public bodies, the last being a dredger completed in 1969. After a succession of short-lived companies repaired ships at the yard, its facilities were demolished in 2007 to provide container storage facilities, an ignominious end to 144 years of ship building and repairing on the Liffey.

Author Pat Sweeney has done an impressive amount of research in Irish newspapers and Irish and UK archives, and this has allowed him to provide considerable detail on the political, commercial and industrial relations background to shipbuilding and repairing in Dublin. There is much on the not always benign influence of the Dublin port authorities. Also discussed are wider events which affected the industry, including independence for Ireland, the resulting civil war and Ireland's controversial neutrality during the Second World War. Sources are noted, there is a glossary and an index. As a paperback the book suffers somewhat from having to cram most of its photographs into a few pages of art paper.

The narrative is interspersed with details of careers of the more significant ships built at Dublin. Although these give colour to what otherwise could have been a simple catalogue of names, their inclusion here tends to distract from the main story. Indeed, a complete list of all Dublin-built vessels would have made an extremely useful appendix, and perhaps an appropriate place for these histories. In some cases the ships' histories have not been researched quite as thoroughly as other aspects of the story. It is noted that the steamer *Mascot* was launched for Norwegian owners by the Dublin Dockyard Company on 28th March 1921, but the author then loses track of her. This is because she was sold to French owners before delivery and renamed *Sainte Marguerite II*. The book then proceeds to treat *Sainte Marguerite II* as the next vessel built by the yard, and gives details of her career, a mistake that would probably have been avoided if a full list of ships with yard numbers had been included. There are also occasional mis-spellings of ships' names such as 'Molfere Rose' for *Moelfre Rose* (repeated in the index).

Overall, however, the author's thorough research into shipbuilding in Dublin has the feel of a lifetime's work, and will be hard to better. His book deserves to do well in informing Dubliners and many others of the ups and downs of an important but often neglected industry in their island nation.

RIVER COLNE SHIPBUILDERS:
A portrait of shipbuilding 1786-1988
John Collins and James Dodds
24.00 x 31.5 cms of 314 pages.
Published by Jardine Press Ltd., 2009.
Softback at £30.00. Hardback with CD at £75.00.
In contrast to the economy displayed by the publishers of the Dublin book, Jardine Press has set out to produce a coffee-

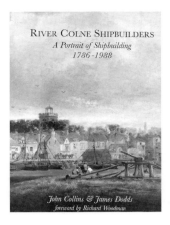

table book. The support of the Heritage Lottery Fund enabled not only publication of the River Colne book, but also liberal use of art paper, illustrations bled to the very edges of the large, two-page spreads and a sprinkling of colour pictures.

Working downriver, locations of yards on the Colne have included Colchester, Rowhedge, Wivenhoe, Brightlingsea and St. Osyth. The best-known of the shipbuilders on the river were Rowhedge Ironworks, and at Wivenhoe Rennie Forrestt, its predecessors, and James W. Cook and Co. Ltd., all of which built coasters, tugs, lighters and small naval craft in iron and steel. However, there are many more yards catalogued in the book, including a number of builders of yachts and other small craft, whose presence makes one quibble over the 'shipbuilders' in the title.

The text provides brief histories of the yards, often supplemented by lengthy extracts from contemporary documents and reminiscences of employees (a significant amount of the research has involved oral history projects). There are fleet list-style entries for sample ships which are shown or discussed. Illustrations include mostly high-quality monochrome photographs (was the use of colour really necessary?) of vessels, yards and occasionally employees; maps; plans; some models and half models; paintings and woodcuts; advertisements and newspaper cuttings. The large format, art paper and generous size and mixture of illustrations make it a very attractive book, although nothing can forgive running superb photographs across a gutter.

Sources are listed, but not annotated, and comprise mainly books of local history and reminiscences plus documents in local record offices. Although there are occasional reproductions of cuttings from newspapers and from technical journals, there appears to have been no systematic search through local newspapers.

The provision of a CD with the hardbook edition promises to solve a major problem of the shipyard historian: how to accommodate intimate details and histories of many hundreds of craft. The amount of work which has gone into the CD is very impressive, and has clearly involved research in shipping registers (mainly those for local ports and for London), in 'Lloyd's Register' and elsewhere. Inevitably details are sparse for many craft which were very small (for instance, dinghies), which went abroad or were generally unrecorded in registers (lighters, pontoons). The perfectionist might expect that more work would have been done on some vessels (for instance, the First World War 'X lighters' which mostly had traceable mercantile careers after the Admiralty finished with them), but the researcher has to call a halt somewhere, and what is provided is very useful.

The book is not just aimed at a largely local market, and the addition of the CD ensures that it is a worthwhile purchase for collectors of shipbuilding histories. Many if not all of the yards dealt with are unlikely to be recorded elsewhere. Readers of 'Record' might find that genuine trading coasters, tugs and sailing vessels are somewhat swamped by pleasure craft, but they will appreciate the many often atmospheric photographs of work in the yards on a variety of wood and steel projects.

Roy Fenton

PORTREATH AND THE BAINS

Tony Pawlyn and Roy Fenton

Although purely coastal shipping has mostly gone from British waters, many small harbours remain as mute testimony to the seafaring activity which was still intense until at least the First World War. Amongst the most poignant of these is the tiny, rock-bound harbour of Portreath in north Cornwall. Taking a coastal steamer through the narrow entrance formed by its stone pier and cliff walls looks to have been an interesting experience with any sort of a blow from the west. To have done the same in a sailing ship speaks volumes for the skills and bravery of crews who did this, year in, year out through the nineteenth century.

Portreath harbour: a brief history

Copper ore from mines in north Cornwall has been shipped out to Swansea and elsewhere since before 1700. In the 18th century copper mining and smelting expanded enormously, and Cornish ore production between 1766 and 1777 exceeded a quarter of a million tons. As well as needing ships to take away the ore, the industry required imports of coal to serve the steam engines which, from their introduction to Cornwall in 1720, helped drain the mines, and to fuel local smelters and crushing machinery.

Portreath Cove provided a convenient and natural, if not always protected, anchorage for vessels serving the major copper mines, being closer than the harbour at Hayle. In 1713 trade was buoyant enough for several local landowners to finance the construction of a quay. One of the major investors was Francis Basset, lord of the manor of Trehidy and local mine owner, resulting in the names Basset's Cove and Basset's Quay being used for the harbour facilities. In 1760 work began to extend the pier, Basset and others now referring to themselves as the Portreath Company. Between 1778 and 1781 Basset's son, another Francis, bought all the shares in the harbour, and proceeded to spend £15,000 on repairs and improvements, including the first basin, built between 1800 and 1805. Some idea of the small size of craft using the port can be had from the widely-quoted statistic that this 280 by 95 foot basin was capable of berthing 25 vessels of about 60 tons burthen. This capacity was no doubt needed: on 22nd March 1805 it was reported that the previous day 28 vessels were lying off Portreath in a heavy ground swell waiting to enter the harbour.

Portreath harbour's trade waxed and waned as copper ore production fluctuated and as transport links were developed. In 1809, it was estimated that 1,000 mule loads were being delivered to the harbour each day. This number of animals would require huge quantities of fodder, the price of which was driven up by the Napoleonic Wars. Clearly, improvements in transport facilities

A deep-laden schooner enters Portreath harbour in calm weather. The stern warp is already fast to the pier and a hobbling boat is taking a bow line. *[Paddy Bradley collection]*

were essential, and between 1809 and 1819 a three-foot gauge plateway - the first in Cornwall - was laid between Portreath and Poldice to serve the North Downs copper mine. This in turn stimulated further improvements to Portreath's facilities, with the pierhead being extended in 1824 and 1825.

However, in 1826 the completion of the four-foot gauge Redruth and Chacewater Railway hurt the harbour's trade, as it allowed ore to be sent out via the port of Devoran to the south, and this coincided with the exhaustion of the North Downs copper mines. Soon, high-grade copper ore from Chile would damage the Cornish mining industry, further harming Portreath's trade. Judging by the recorded harbour dues, coal imports were now more important than ore exports and in 1836 a total of 347 vessels over 50 tons entered the harbour, of which 83 were in ballast and 264 brought in coal and other cargoes.

A branch line of the standard-gauge Hayle Railway reached Portreath via an inclined plane in 1838, and this connection with the mines around Camborne revitalised the harbour's trade. This necessitated an inner basin, work on which began in 1846. Seen in many of the accompanying photographs, this was smaller than the existing basin. Of 200 by 100 feet, it would be capable of 'conveniently receiving and containing ten additional vessels'. Other facilities were improved, including provision of railway sidings, coal yards and ore hutches. In June 1851 the first steamer entered Portreath Harbour, the *Augusta* (149/1849) arriving with coal from Llanelly 'in good style', according to the 'West Briton'. However, the claim that Portreath was then 'one of the most important ports in Cornwall' seems an exaggeration, given its size.

In anything like a blow, entering or leaving Portreath harbour could be an interesting experience for a crew. Here Bain's *Feadon* punches her way into a sloppy sea past Burrel's Quarry. Despite the weather, there are a number of onlookers. *[Paddy Bradley collection]*

The schooner *Chrysolite* (128/1869) was typical of sailing vessels trading to Portreath, although not owned by Bains. In the background of this photograph in Penzance floating dock, is *Plover* yet to receive Bain's funnel markings. *[Tony Pawlyn collection]*

The Redruth and Chacewater Railway was converted to steam haulage in 1855 and this led to another, and final, decline in Portreath's exports as Hayle and Devoran were better placed for shipping out ore. This was also the year Cornwall's copper ore production peaked at almost 210,000 tons, and thereafter it declined, precipitously so from 1865. The Poldice Tramroad declined along with the mines it served, although it was still used intermittently until at least 1885. However, Portreath remained comparatively important for the import of coal destined for the mines. In 1866, 60,000 tons of coal passed through Portreath, whilst Devoran handled 66,000 tons and Hayle 70,000 tons.

The Bain family
The later fortunes of the harbour at Portreath were closely entwined with those of the Bain family. Donald Bain (1774-1850) was a native of Wick in Caithness who was attracted by the prosperity of the mining industry and moved to West Cornwall in the late eighteenth century. Although he initially taught at Redruth Grammar School, in 1809 his arithmetical accomplishments saw him engaged to run the estate office of the Williams family of Scorrier, who had extensive interests in copper mining and related industries. From 1826, the Williams and others leased the harbour at Portreath, and in 1831 Donald Bain was transferred there as chief cashier.

Although Portreath harbour remained in the ownership of the Bassett family, by the time of Donald Bain's death in 1850 he appears to have obtained effective control of the port, and his son David Wise Bain became harbour master that year. The Bain family's money was invested widely, in many of the Cornish mines, in a tin smelter at Redruth (along with tin mines in Malaya), the Redruth and District Bank, and the West Cornwall Steamship

The iron, three-masted *Penwith* was built for Bains by Harvey and Co. of Hayle in 1878. Her career was short: she disappeared after leaving Penarth in December 1880. *[Tony Pawlyn collection]*

Co. Ltd. Bains also built up a fleet of coastal sailing vessels and later steamers.

The sailing fleet
The sailing ships were managed by David Wise Bain, with local shareholders who included himself, his brother Richard Bain and his father-in-law Martin Hitchens of St. Austell. Their first sailing ship is believed to have been the wooden schooner *Ellen Vair*, built for them at Boscastle in 1858. As the table 1 overleaf shows, the growth of the sail fleet was impressive. New and second-hand schooners and barquentines of wood, composite and iron construction arrived in (and in many cases departed from) the fleet at intervals until 20 ships had passed through Bain's hands by 1890. What is also impressive is the family's fortitude in the face of the frequent losses to which any fleet of coastal sail was vulnerable. Ten - fully half of all their sailing ships - were lost; whilst at least five others came to violent ends after their sale to other owners. David Bain had the reputation of being an efficient but not ruthless manager of ships and men. For instance, he insisted that his masters insured their lives, and paid half of their premiums himself.

Despite the intense rivalry between Portreath and Hayle, Bain clearly had a high regard for the shipbuilding of Harvey and Co. Between 1864 and 1878, he had five ships built by their Hayle yard:

Eliza Bain	1864/176	Composite schooner
Ellen Vair	1866/137	Wooden schooner
Western Wave	1866/229	Composite schooner
Millie Bain	1872/248	Wooden brigantine
Penwith	1878/289	Iron barquentine

Shipbuilding is recorded at Portreath at least as early as 1843, but is best documented later in the 19th century. Michael Tangye lists 11 wooden sailing vessels built at Portreath between 1867 and 1884, all in the name of shipwright Thomas Massey. Surprisingly, given his close involvement with the port, Bain had an interest in only one, the schooner *Tregea* of 1877, which traded to the Mediterranean.

Details of losses and other records confirm that, despite their small size, David Bain's sailing ships often traded well beyond home trade limits. His iron brigantine *Penair* went to South America for hides, to the West Indies, to the Mediterranean for citrus fruit and currants, and to Spain for iron ore. The iron *Belle of Lagos* and *Thomas Blythe* ran in the nitrate trade to Chile, taking out Welsh coal or occasionally mining machinery made in Hayle. In 1873 the *Ellen Vair* made a voyage from Antwerp to Santander and at the latter port the body of her young master, Richard Gregory of Hayle, was found floating in the river, although whether this was the result of an accident or an attempt at robbery was never discovered.

The Harvey-built *Penwith* was a fine, iron-hulled barquentine, and disappeared after sailing from Penarth Dock with coal for Rio Grande do Sul on 10th May 1880. During the enquiry into her loss, some evidence was presented about the sobriety of her master, but most discussion concerned the coal cargo, its stowage, trimming, gaseous nature and lack of hold ventilation. The presiding magistrate concluded that there was nothing in the evidence to suggest that the master, the officers or crew were not sober or competent to navigate the ship when she sailed from Penarth Dock. No opinion was offered on the cause of loss.

As larger iron sailing vessels and steamers began to take more of the longer distance trades, the small sailing ships in the Bain fleet tended to work more in home trades. There were accidents here too: on 1st February 1883 the *Storm Nymph* was bringing coal from Cardiff into Hayle when she ran on to the beach east of the harbour. All but one of the crew were taken off by rocket life-saving apparatus. The *English Maid* was also on a local voyage, bringing coal from Newport, when she ran ashore at the entrance to Portreath harbour on 6th April 1887. Her crew landed by boat, but the wooden schooner's bottom was 'knocked out' and she became a total loss.

Sailing ships in which Bains had an interest. All are wood unless stated.

Name	In fleet	Rig	O.N.	Built	Dimensions (feet)	Tonnages	Fate/disposal
Ellen Vair (1)	1858-1864	Schooner	27391	1864 by George, Boscastle	80.2 x 21.5 x 11.3	116g 116n	17.11.1864 foundered.
Trio	1861-1893	Schooner	23001	1861 at Walsoken	71.0 x 21.0 x 11.3	103g 103n	1893 broken up.
English Maid	1861-1887	Schooner	15866	1856 by Peterhead Ship. Co., Perth	85.7 x 21.4 x 11.3	119g 119n	6.4.1887 wrecked at Portreath whilst on voyage Newport to Portreath, coal
Glenfeadon	1863-1908	Schooner	47005	1863 by Hodge, Pill	92.5 x 21.7 x 11.4	128g 99n	1908 sold.
Eliza Bain	1864-1898	Schooner	49982	1864 by Harvey & Co., Hayle	106.6 x 24.3 x 12.0	176g 176n	1898 sold. 27.11.1902 wrecked at Sunderland, from Teignmouth with clay.
Saint Agnes (1)	1865-1868	Schooner	49983	1865 by Harvey & Co., Hayle	107.8 x 24.7 x 12.2	176g 176n	1868 lost.
Ellen Vair (2)	1866-1893	Schooner	49988	1866 by Harvey & Co., Hayle	95.4 x 22.2 x 12.0	137g 107n	1893 went missing.
Western Wave	1866-1874	Composite three-masted schooner	49990	1866 by Harvey & Co., Hayle	118.5 x 23.5 x 12.9	229g 229n	2.4.1874 left Lisbon for Hull and disappeared.
Thomas Blythe	1866-1881	Iron brigantine	27648	1859 by Smith & Co., Preston	137.2 x 25.0 x 16.6	382g 382n	6.8.1881 foundered North Atlantic whilst on voyage Samanco, Peru to Liverpool, sugar.
Bessie	1867-1888	Schooner	44899	1863 by Butson, Polruan	99.5 x 22.0 x 12.0	152g 144n	4.6.1888 wrecked St. Aubin, France whilst on voyage Cardiff to Trouville, coal.
Sarah Fox	1868-1887	Schooner	58672	1868 by Lelean, Megavissey	87.5 x 22.8 x 11.8	134g 121n	1887 sold. 14.11.1891 wrecked at Sunderland, from South Shields, scrap.
Storm Nymph	1868-1883	Schooner	4614	1854 at Arbroath	89.4 x 21.4 x 10.9	126g 113n	1.2.1883 wrecked Hayle, whilst on voyage Cardiff to Hayle, coal.
Margaret	1868-1888	Iron three-masted schooner	49986	1866 by Vivian Sandys & Carne, Copper House, Hayle.	127.6 x 25.7 x 11.1	232g 216n	10.5.1888 collided with steamer *Risca* (689/1866) near East Goodwin L.V., whilst on voyage Rotterdam to Penzance, straw.
Queen of the Sea	1871-1895	Schooner	14145	1852 by Thomas Waters, Bideford	82.5 x 19.7 x 8.4	130g 110n	1895 sold. 2.11.1898 wrecked near Dungeness, Tyne to Exeter, coal.
Millie Bain	1872-1896	Brigantine	58678	1872 by Harvey & Co., Hayle	124.4 x 25.2 x 13.4	249g 232n	1896 sold. 9.11.1904 foundered near Haaks L.V., Antwerp to Newcastle, sand.
Tregea	1873-1898	Schooner	58679	1872 by Thomas Massey, Portreath	98.4 x 24.9 x 11.1	158g 145n	1898 sold. 13.11.1905 sailed Glasgow for Lanion with coal and disappeared.
Penair	1874-1887	Iron brigantine	29733	1862 by Vivian Sandys & Carne, Copper House, Hayle	113.8 x 23.7 x 12.0	212g 189n	c 11.11.1887 stranded Hogland, Gulf of Finland whilst on voyage St Petersburg to Elsinore.
Penwith	1878-1880	Iron brigantine	68866	1878 by Harvey & Co., Hayle	137.4 x 26.2 x 12.5	289g 276n	11.5.1880 sailed Cardiff for Rio Grande do Sul with coal and disappeared.
Belle of Lagos	1878-1890	Iron brigantine	60092	1868 by A. Stephen, Kelvinhaugh	130.7 x 25.1 x 11.4	244g 228n	6.1890 sold to German owners.
Saint Agnes (2)	1888-1891*	Schooner	58680	1872 by Hitchins, St Agnes	66.0 x 20.2 x 9.0	63g 58n	1905 sold.

* Bain was executor only.

The steam fleet

By the 1880s Bains' fleet of small sailing ships was feeling competition from steamers in the coastal trades and no sailing ships were added after 1878. David Bain is believed to have been persuaded by his son Frederick that the future lay with coastal steam ships, but the story is probably more complex. In 1886 Gustavus Basset, the current owner of Portreath harbour, declared it an 'open port', ceasing to charge harbour dues. He also insisted on a 'coal clause' that attempted to make mines in which he had an interest ship their coal exclusively through Portreath. This caused friction with the larger port of Hayle, a few miles to the south west, where the ship building and engineering company Harvey and Co. was already running a small fleet of coastal steamers, but was probably instrumental in the Bains' decision to embrace steam. It is hardly a coincidence that steam cranes were installed at Portreath in 1888. These would expedite the unloading of steamers although, as several of the accompanying photographs show, manual unloading also continued for many years. The acquisition of the steam tug, *Portreath*, in 1888 indicates that sailing ships remained important to the port.

Bain's first steamer, *Veronica*, was bought from Cardiff owners in 1887, followed by the *Olivia* which had been, rather unusually, built in South Wales. The steam fleet expanded in the early 1890s, with the *Treleigh* being notable as the first new steamer to be ordered by the family. She was followed by the new *Guardian*, slightly larger but with her bridge amidships. Her name derived from David Bain's position on the Redruth Board of Guardians which administered the local workhouse. One wonders at his motives for such a choice: did he want to remind his crews of where they might end up if they did not work hard? *Guardian* came from a builder in Inverkeithing more experienced at constructing fishing vessels than cargo ships. Her engines by Clyne, Mitchell and Co. of Aberdeen were unreliable: she was frequently disabled by breakdowns and became known as the 'hospital ship' because of the periods she spent laid up at Portreath.

All other steamers acquired came second-hand, and were often of some antiquity. For instance, *Lynx* was 24-years old on arriving in 1893, having been briefly owned by members of the Williams family of Scorrier who have already been referred to as having mining interests locally. *Feadon* was 26 years old,

Bain's *Olivia* is towed out of Portreath harbour by *Panmure* about 1898. Once again the pier head has proved a popular place for villagers to assemble. *[Paddy Bradley collection]*

The first new steamer ordered by David Bain was the *Treleigh* of 1894. Crowds on both quayside watch her on Portreath's western wharf (middle): could this be her maiden arrival at Portreath in January 1894? Beyond her, the baulk crane has completed closing the basin. Baulks were first used in 1839, it is said to protect vessels in the basin from heavy seas, but they may well have been used to trap water so that vessels remained afloat whilst discharging. The crane dates from 1859. The black 'B' for Bain on the yellow band of her otherwise black funnel was made of metal. Note the scrap of sail furled to her mizzen mast in the bottom photograph, all that remains of the full suit she would have carried when new. *[Both: Paddy Bradley collection]*

A delightful view of Portreath's dock basins looking down from Lighthouse Hill. Nearest the camera is *Olivia* discharging coal. On the other side of the outer basin, *Treleigh* waits with her hatch boards off, whilst two members of her crew take advantage of the low water to do some painting. In the inner basin, *Guardian* is also discharging coal. The rope-worked inclined plane of the railway to Portreath can be seen beyond the harbour. Its 1-in-10 incline functioned as late as 1932. During the Second World War the rails were removed and a concrete wall constructed across its base. *[Paddy Bradley collection]*

acquired after an accident in 1893 and renamed after the Bain's home. Although *Coniston Fell* was just 12, she was followed by a real veteran, the 41-year-old *Panmure*. The steamers' funnels were painted black with a particularly broad yellow band, on which was a black letter B. No house flag is known, and Bain probably disdained such a frippery.

At much the same time as the steam fleet was expanding, 'Lloyd's Register' began listing the owners as Bain, Sons and Co. rather than simply as David W. Bain, suggesting that Frederick and his brothers Arthur and John were gradually taking over. Frederick Donald Bain's middle name came from his grandfather, and like his forebears he is reputed have been bluff, vigorous and multi-talented. David Bain died in July 1898, from which date his sons exerted full control.

Casualties often cluster distressingly, and the years 1899 and 1900 saw the first total losses amongst the steamer fleet. On 1st October 1899 *Lynx* was wrecked near Port Isaacs whilst outward bound from Portreath in ballast. Less than two months later, on 29th November 1899, *Coniston Fell* sank in a collision in the River Mersey whilst carrying cement from the Thames. In April 1900 another collision resulted in the *Veronica* sinking off Hartland Point. The run of ill-luck came to an end in March 1904 when off Swanscombe in the Thames a third collision saw the *Feadon* survive but fit only for scrap.

Well built for the Whitehaven owners W.S. Kennaugh and Co., *Holme Wood* was acquired in 1905 when already 22 years old. She seems to have been a favourite of Frederick Bain, possibly because she was relatively fast and with a draught of less than nine feet could use small harbours. Crews of other Bain steamers complained that, unlike their ships, *Holme Wood* 'was never in for a weekend away'. Bain had a reputation for greeting a master arriving at Portreath with the words 'All right, Captain, get you together, you're away up north again'.

Another arrival in 1905 was the somewhat younger *Test*, a mere 15 years old. In later life – she survived for 56 years – Test was commanded by Captain Owen Spargo. In the marvellous book which Owen co-authored, 'Old Time Steam Coasting', he described *Test* as being like 'an armchair' she was so comfortable. She was also very strongly built, although he notes that the pounding she had often taken in rough weather left her with 'a good many soft spots'. *Test* was Bain's last acquisition, and from 1912 the coasters began to be sold.

Voyage patterns

Crew agreements give snapshots of where Bains' ships were working. During the second half of 1894 *Treleigh* visited Portreath eight times on voyages that had begun at the coal ports of Garston (four times), Point of Ayr (twice), Lydney and Neath. Another visit

Guardian discharging coal on the eastern wharf. A dockside steam crane is working the fore hold, whilst the after hold is being discharged largely by muscle power: the coal is being raised to a plank from where it is barrowed ashore. *[Paddy Bradley collection]*

Holme Wood having just brought another coal cargo to the eastern wharf in Portreath's outer basin (above left), and preparing to leave the turning basin for sea whilst her stern rope is retrieved (below left). *Holme Wood* was registered in Hull in 1889, and Bain never bothered to reregister her locally (above right). *[Above right: World Ship Society Ltd., others: Paddy Bradley collection]*

Treleigh in Holman's dry dock, Penzance, where the Bain fleet was routinely repaired and surveyed. Built of iron when this material had largely been replaced by steel 'Rolling Reggie' gave Bains 30 years of service. *[Tony Pawlyn collection]*

to Garston was to load coal for Tralee. A total of three visits were made to Neath, and two each to Newport, Lydney, Point of Ayr, Lancaster, Cork and – surprisingly – Rouen. Single visits were made to Mistley, London, Rochester, Newhaven, Fowey, Pengarth, Burry Port, Passage West, Waterford, Tralee, Silloth, Kirkcudbright and Manchester – the last-named probably to the Ship Canal which was not opened as far as Manchester until 1895. A total of 40 passages were made in the six months, averaging 2.4 days at sea, the longest being an eight-day voyage to Neath in November during which she must have been weather-bound. A total of 70 days were spent in port, the longest stays being five days in each of London and Mistley. Loading at Point of Ayr was particularly brisk, *Treleigh* arriving on one tide on 23rd September and leaving on the next. Judging by the loading ports, coal was absolutely predominant. Stone cargoes were also taken to ports in the south east, where a cargo of cement might be loaded for the north east or whiting for the north west.

The other ships whose crew agreements have been sampled were much more frequent visitors to Portreath. During the first six months of 1889, *Olivia* called on 44 occasions, also making single calls at Hayle, Devoran and Truro. She mostly loaded at Neath (25 voyages), but also at Porthcawl (eight), Lydney (six), Newport (five), Port Talbot (three) and Cardiff. With the exception of the one visit to Truro, she traded solely within the Bristol Channel, reflected in her making 95 passages, of an average of 0.92 days. Coal from Lydney in the Forest of Dean might be consigned to Redruth Brewery and on occasion would consist of a mixture of sizes described as 'manor coal' because it was destined for Tehidy Manor.

In the whole of 1901 *Panmure* called at Portreath 34 times, although otherwise her pattern was not dissimilar to that of *Treleigh* seven years earlier. With eleven visits, Neath narrowly beat Garston and Newport (ten each), and Lydney (six). Small South Welsh ports visited included Burry Port, Pembrey, Porthcawl and Saundersfoot. Calls at Plymouth, Par and Fowey were to load china clay for Runcorn. The most distant ports visited were Greenock once and Newcastle on three occasions. Two visits to the Tyne were made when voyages from Portreath had

The oldest vessel in what was generally a mature fleet, *Panmure* had been bought by Bains from the War Department in 1900 and registered at Penzance. She was photographed in the Bristol Channel after her sale by Bain in 1912, when she went first to London owners, and then passed through a number of hands until broken up in 1924, by when she was 65 years old. *[J. and M. Clarkson]*

taken the *Panmure* to the East Coast and at least one – coal from Newcastle to Wexford – might have taken the old steamer north round Scotland. Single visits were made to Dublin, Belfast, Hull, Grimsby and Kings Lynn.

Treleigh

The late Clive Carter has written about Bain's *Treleigh* from the reminiscences of those who crewed her, who referred to her as 'Rolling Reggie' after her behaviour in bad weather. Her first crew of ten was signed on at her builder's yard on Tyneside on 20th January 1894, six days before she was registered, to bring her round to Portreath. Several crew members came from Bain's other steamers, *Olivia* or *Lynx*, and some from local sailing ships. Of her two firemen, the 15-year old James Reynolds deserted at Fenit, forfeiting his wages rather than going back to sea in *Treleigh*. The articles her crew signed required the deck hands and firemen to assist each other when required, and to help work the cargo if necessary. On a number of occasions miners joined the crews of Bain's ships, swapping a hard life underground for an equally rigorous one in the open air: all of the coasters had open bridges.

Berthed in the *Treleigh's* forecastle, the seamen and firemen might find that the door burst open in rough weather, leaving the lower bunks awash and putting out the coal stove. Food was usually cooked in the tiny galley under the port wing of the bridge and had to be carried forward across the open deck to the forecastle, a hazardous journey in rough weather. Not surprisingly, the conditions on *Treleigh*, the meagre pay and her modest speed meant she often sailed short-handed.

Treleigh had several near disasters when entering Portreath, including an incident in October 1896 when she was driven into Burrel's Quarry alongside the harbour. Backing out she sank, completely blocking the harbour entrance. After her coal was unloaded she was raised and repaired, probably at Holman's dry dock at Penzance, where Bain's coasters were regularly docked, surveyed and patched up.

Treleigh was one of many coasters to be requisitioned in the First World War (she was the only Bain steamer to be called up) and is believed to have carried coal for the Admiralty, and to have had the luxury of a six-pounder gun. Her master William Connett was awarded the British Empire Medal for his wartime service in *Treleigh*. Returned to Bain in March 1919, she was practically rebuilt in Holman's dry dock at Penzance. Although there would be plenty of work for her with the general shortage of ships in the immediate post-war period, the coasting trade never completely recovered after the war and, with the closure of the biggest mines around Camborne, local trades were particularly hard hit. Symptomatic of conditions in Cornwall, during the winter of 1921 *Treleigh* gave unemployed miners free passages to South Wales to look for work.

Finale

Sale of the *Test* in 1915 and *Guardian* in 1916 left Bains with just four steamers, and wartime hazards were soon to halve the fleet. Despite Royal Navy patrols, German submarines penetrated the Irish Sea on several occasions, and on 11th February 1917 the *UC 65* captured the *Olivia* just off Bardsey whilst the coaster was heading home with a coal cargo from Garston. *Olivia's* crew took

A laden *Treleigh* appears to be aground in the outer basin at Portreath, with part of her crew posing for the camera on her stern rail and a hobbler's boat in the foreground. *[Paddy Bradley collection]*

Sailing carefully from Portreath, *Guardian* is watched by spectators in their best clothes. *[Paddy Bradley collection]*

to their boat, nearly forgetting the 80-year old chief engineer who was still asleep in his bunk. Once he was on board and wrapped in his greatcoat, the boat was rowed over to the submarine. The frightened crew were taken on to the casing and were given the somewhat limited assurance that they were safe unless a British patrol boat appeared. Once *Olivia* had been sunk, the crew were put back into their boat, from which they were picked up by the Ellerman steamer *City of Bristol* (6,741/1912) and landed at Fishguard. Here the manager of the station buffet was persuaded to give them a hot breakfast before they were sent home to Cornwall in a carriage specially attached to the rear of a Plymouth-bound goods train.

Extinguishing of lights on ships was a wartime hazard which ended the life of *Plover*. In May 1918 she was bound across the Bristol Channel when rammed by the darkened Norwegian steamer *Lesseps*. The *Plover* slowly capsized in a calm sea, all

but one of the crew jumping into the water and managing to stay afloat with the help of hatch boards washed off the coaster. They were picked up by a steamer, identified as the Guinness-owned *Carrowdore* (599/1914), which also recovered the body of *Plover's* chief engineer. Survivors were transferred to a sailing lugger off Godrevy.

The fleet available to the Bains was now reduced to just *Holme Wood*, which herself got aground on Hayle Bar late in 1918, and went to Penzance for repairs where she was joined by the war-weary *Treleigh* on her release from Admiralty service. Once the immediate post-war boom in freights had blown itself out, finding profitable work for ageing steam coasters was almost impossible. Both Bains' steamers staggered on until 1924 when Frederick Bain retired. *Holme Wood* went for scrap after being damaged whilst berthed at Portreath but *Treleigh* found a new local owner in James Bawden. Although *Treleigh* survived for another seven years, her condition must have been parlous, as whilst undergoing survey at Falmouth in 1931 a weight sank through her rusty fore deck. Later that year she was sold and broken up at Lelant.

This was by no means the end of shipping at Portreath. The harbour was first leased to the County of Cornwall Shipping Co. Ltd. of Redruth, which had built up a fleet of steam coasters since its formation in 1919. It then passed to Arthur Reynolds, who had emigrated from Camborne to the Transvaal and prospered before returning home, and who began acquiring steam coasters in 1929. Four ships passed through the ownership of Reynolds, the last Portreath ship owner, before he too gave up in 1938. The final holder of the lease was the Beynon Shipping Co. Ltd. based in Cardiff. Its small steamer *Islesman* (281/1904), bought from Reynolds in 1938, was photographed several times in Portreath before she was sold to breakers at the end of 1954. Tangye claims that British vessels then refused to enter the harbour, and its trade was left to Dutch vessels, the last of which called about 1960.

A post-Second World War view from Lighthouse Hill of the *Islesman* departing Portreath. Formerly owned in Portreath by Arthur Reynolds, Islesman was now in the ownership of Beynon Shipping Co. Ltd. of Cardiff. She still has an open bridge, which she probably retained until sold to Dutch shipbreakers and demolished at Nieuwe Lekkerland in 1955. *[Paddy Bradley collection]*

Steamer fleet list

1. VERONICA 1887-1900 Iron
O.N. 86495 255g 135n
120.6 x 23.5 x 9.8 feet
C. 2-cyl. by Plenty and Son, Newbury; 40 NHP.
12.1882: Completed by Charles Hill and Sons, Bristol (Yard No. 3).
13.1.1883: Registered in the ownership of John Cuthbert and John Hancock, Cardiff as VERONICA.
1884: Transferred to John Hancock and Co., Cardiff.
3.1887: Acquired by David W. Bain and Co., Portreath.

22.4.1900: Lost in collision with the steamer GLYNN (1,106/1899) six miles north east of Hartland Point whilst on a voyage from Portreath to Lydney in ballast. The crew of seven reached Padstow in the ship's boat.
8.5.1900: Register closed.

2. OLIVIA 1888-1917 Iron
O.N. 86742 242g 128n
121.0 x 22.2 x 9.8 feet
C. 2-cyl. by Sheryn and Laurie, Newport; 40 NHP.
1.1883: Launched by Mordey, Carney and Co. Ltd., Newport (Yard No.7).
24.2.1883: Registered in the ownership

of William Hunter and Co., Glasgow as OLIVIA.
1886: Sold to Bell Brothers and McLelland, Glasgow.
1886: Transferred to the Olivia Steamship Co. Ltd. (Bell Brothers and McLelland, managers), Glasgow.
1888: Acquired by David W. Bain and Co., Portreath.
11.2.1917: Captured and sunk by bombs by the German submarine UC 65 21 miles south west half south of Bardsey Island whilst on a voyage from Garston to Portreath with a cargo of coal. The crew was landed at Fishguard.
25.2.1917: Register closed.

3. LYNX 1893-1899 Iron

O.N. 58864 132g 72n
104.0 x 20.2 x 8.6 feet
1870: 163g 111n
124.0 x 20.3 x 8.6 feet
2-cyl. by Joy and Co., Middlesbrough; 35 NHP.
6.1869: Launched by Backhouse and Dixon, Middlesbrough (Yard No. 39).
26.6.1869: Registered in the ownership of Frederick Williams (32/64) and James O. Purves (32/64), Middlesbrough as LYNX.
1870: Lengthened, probably by the builder.
1871: Sold to William R.J. Hopkins, Middlesbrough.
1872: Sold to Joseph Robinson, Middlesex.
29.11.1892: Acquired by Michael Henry Williams, John Williams and Percival D. Williams, Redruth following a high court order.
7.1.1893: Acquired by David W. Bain and Co., Portreath.
1.10.1899: Wrecked at Bounds Cliff three miles east of Port Isaac whilst on a voyage from Portreath to Port Talbot in ballast.
27.10.1899: Register closed.

4. TRELEIGH 1894-1924 Iron

O.N. 96564 347g 174n
140.0 x 23.6 x 9.7 feet
C. 2-cyl. by J.P. Rennoldson and Sons, South Shields; 45 NHP, 270 IHP, 9 knots.
1.1894: Completed by J.P. Rennoldson and Sons, South Shields (Yard No. 155).
26.1.1894: Registered in the ownership of David W. Bain and Co., Portreath as TRELEIGH.
7.12.1898: Owners became Frederick D. Bain and Arthur P. Bain, Portreath.
3.10.1924: Sold to James R. Bawden, Redruth.
9.12.1931: Breaking up began by T.W. Ward Ltd. of Sheffield at Lelant, Cornwall.
11.3.1932: Register closed.

5. FEADON 1894-1904 Iron

O.N. 56069 269g 182n
130.2 x 24.8 x 12.6 feet
1873: 293g 187n
140.5 x 25.1 x 10.6 feet
1894: 269g 109n
2-cyl. by Palmer's Shipbuilding and Iron Co. Ltd., Jarrow; 45 NHP.
1867: Launched by Palmer's Shipbuilding and Iron Co. Ltd., Jarrow (Yard No. 218).
22.8.1867: Registered in the ownership of Palmer's Shipbuilding and Iron Co. Ltd., Jarrow as GRINKLE.
1873: Lengthened, probably by the builders.
12.12.1893: Sank following a collision in the Tyne.
1.2.1894: Register closed.
7.5.1894: Registered in the ownership of David W. Bain and Co., Portreath as GRINKLE.
19.6.1894: Renamed FEADON.
12.3.1904: In collision with the steamer NORTHUMBRIA (872/1869) off Bell Wharf, Swanscombe in the River Thames whilst on a voyage from London to

Feadon discharges at the pier in the original part of Portreath harbour, also known as the turning basin, about 1895. Note the precarious arrangement of planks and trestles necessary to unload her into wheelbarrows, whilst a steam crane stands idly by. Gull Rock is seen in the background. *[Cornwall Studies Library]*

Judging by her plain black funnel with the letter 'B' removed, these photographs of *Treleigh* at Preston were taken after her sale to James R. Bawden of Redruth in 1924. She probably still ran coal to Portreath on occasion until sold for scrap in 1931. *[World Ship Society Limited]*

Lancaster with a cargo of whiting. The crew was saved.
Later condemned. The wreck was sold to Blackmore, Gould and Co., London for breaking up.
17.8.1904: Register closed.

6. CONISTON FELL 1895-1899

O.N. 86265 337g 130n
144.6 x 22.0 x 10.0 feet
C. 2-cyl. by David Rollo and Sons, Liverpool; 65 NHP.
7.1882: Launched by H. Tipping and Co., Portsmouth.
12.12.1882: Registered in the ownership of the Coniston Fell Steam Ship Co. Ltd. (Hume, Smith and Co., managers), Liverpool as CONISTON FELL.
13.3.1886: Managers became George Nelson

and Sons, Whitehaven and later Liverpool.
28.3.1894: Manager became William L. Jackson, Liverpool.
2.10.1894: Acquired by David W. Bain and Co., Portreath.
29.11.1899: Sank off New Brighton pier in the River Mersey following a collision with the steamer SULLY (1,326/1874) whilst on a voyage from London to Birkenhead with a cargo of cement.
14.12.1899: Register closed.

7. GUARDIAN 1896-1916

O.N. 96565 381g 162n
146.0 x 23.7 x 9.3 feet
C. 2-cyl. by Clyne, Mitchell and Co., Aberdeen; 64 NHP, 457 IHP, 9.5 knots.
8.1896: Completed by Cumming and Ellis, Inverkeithing (Yard No.23).

3.9.1896: Registered in the ownership of David W. Bain, trading as Bain, Sons and Co., Portreath as GUARDIAN.
7.12.1898: Transferred to Frederick D. Bain, John H. Bain and Arthur P. Bain, Portreath.
2.2.1916: Sold to Cunningham, Shaw and Co. Ltd. (Vernon Shaw Lovell, manager), London.
16.10.1916: Sold to The Cheviot Coasters Ltd. (George T. Gillie and Co., managers), Newcastle-upon-Tyne.
28.10.1920: Transferred to George T. Gillie, John A. Blair and Mowbray Thompson, Newcastle-upon-Tyne.
11.4.1923: Transferred to Northumbria Transports Ltd. (George T. Gillie and Co., managers), Newcastle-upon-Tyne.
12.4.1924: Transferred to the Home Trade Shipping Co. Ltd. (George T. Gillie and Co. (Glasgow) Ltd., managers), Glasgow.
16.12.1924: Sold to Arthur T. Walker, York and Ivan A. Dernier, South Shields.
18.3.1925: Transferred to the Walker-Dernier Steamship Co. Ltd., Hull (Arthur T. Walker, York, manager).
26.8.1925: Manager became George T. Gillie and Co., Newcastle-upon-Tyne (on behalf of mortgagees, the Home Trade Shipping Co. Ltd.).
14.1.1926: Sold by mortgagees to the Freear and Dix Steam Shipping Co. Ltd. (Ernest F. Dix, manager), Sunderland.
27.10.1927: Manager became George T. Gillie and Co., Newcastle-upon-Tyne (on behalf of mortgagees, the Home Trade Shipping Co. Ltd.).
29.11.1927: Foundered after springing a leak six miles east south east of the North Goodwin Light Vessel whilst on a voyage from Ghent to London with a cargo of rails. Her crew escaped in a boat and rowed to the North Goodwin Light Vessel, from where they were taken ashore by the Ramsgate Lifeboat.
21.12.1927: Register closed.

8. PANMURE 1900-1912 Iron
O.N. 96567 321g 129n
148.2 x 22.0 x 12.0 feet
1883: C. 2-cyl. by Seaward and Co., Millwall.
1859: Launched by J. and W. Dudgeon, Limehouse, London for the Secretary of State for War, London as LORD PANMURE.
5.10.1900: Registered in the ownership of John H. Bain, Frederick D. Bain and Arthur P. Bain, trading as Bain, Sons and Co., Portreath as PANMURE.
2.10.1912: Sold to Harry Barnett, London.
25.9.1916: Sold to John Goldstein, Alexander M. Jones and Frederick Andrews (Copeland K. Etheridge, manager), London.
16.10.1916: Transferred to Jones, Grainger and Co. (Etheridge and Cockerell, managers), London.
11.9.1918: Sold to the Panmure Steam Ship Co. Ltd. (Tom W. Smyth, manager), London.
12.7.1920: Sold to The Spanish and General Corporation Ltd. (Hubert W. Corby, manager), London.

A possibly unique view of the engines-amidships *Coniston Fell* in the outer basin in 1898. The steamer to her right, with a gaff on her mainmast and two broadly spaced white rings on her funnel, has not been identified. *[Francis Frith 41628]*

Guardian at Bristol during Bains' ownership. The masts and derricks are varnished, and the canvas dodger on her bridge shining white. Note also the piece of canvas on her forestay. Regarded as unreliable during Bains' ownership, *Guardian* changed hands frequently between her sale in 1916 and her loss in 1927. *[J. and M. Clarkson]*

30.11.1920: Sold to Carreg-y-Llam Quarries Ltd. (August S. Birch, manager), London.
27.10.1924: Register closed, the vessel having been broken up.

9. PLOVER 1900-1918 Iron
O.N. 96038 277g 115n
140.0 x 22.1 x 10.5 feet
C. 2-cyl. by Hutton and Corbett, Glasgow.
1.12.1888: Launched by John Fullerton and Co., Paisley (Yard No. 83).
2.1.1889: Registered in the ownership of Henry Burton, Newport as PLOVER.

20.6.1898: Transferred to R. Burton and Son Ltd., Cardiff.
14.7.1900: Acquired by Bain, Sons and Co., Portreath.
11.5.1909: Struck Gullard Rock, off Padstow, in fog.
11.5.1918: Sunk in collision with the Norwegian steamer LESSEPS (1,747/1881) seven miles north by a quarter west of Hartland Point, in position 51.11.30 north, 04.31.45 west, whilst on a voyage from Portreath to Saundersfoot in ballast. One member of the crew was lost.
3.6.1918: Register closed.

179

In September 1908, *Panmure* entered Holman's dry dock at Penzance to have a new stern frame and tail shaft fitted. This sequence of photographs begins with the stern frame being lowered into the dry dock (right).

The stern frame is offered up - note the bevelled end to the keel iron (middle left).

The photograph bottom left shows the stern frame waiting to be driven home: note the alignment of the drill holes with the rivet holes in the shell plating.

An oscillating reamer is used to fair up the tail shaft (top right), with power provided by an early steam engine on the dockside (middle right).

The finished job (right): note the second-hand propellor, cut down to fit.

Panmure left Penzance on 22nd October 1908, 34 days after arriving. Perhaps surprisingly, after all this work, she was sold in 1912. *[All: Percy Holman/Tony Pawlyn collection]*

10. HOLME WOOD 1905-1924
Iron

O.N. 84636 229g 90n
130.0 x 21.2 x 8.8 feet
C. 2-cyl. by J. and T. Young, Ayr.

7.1883: Launched by R. Williamson and Son, Workington (Yard No.77).
29.8.1883: Registered in the ownership of William S. Kennaugh and Co., Whitehaven as SCALE FORCE.
7.1891: Sold to R. Williamson and Son, Workington.
1894: Renamed HOLME WOOD.
23.12.1899: Sold to William H.H. Hutchinson, Hull.
25.10.1904: Sold to the South Coast Steamship Co. (1904) Ltd. (Kennedy, Collingwood and Co., managers), London.
24.10.1905: Acquired by Bain, Sons and Co., Portreath.
1924: Sold to British shipbreakers.
5.11.1924: Register closed.

11. TEST 1905-1915

O.N. 93227 530g 209n
175.0 x 26.5 x 10.1 feet
T. 3-cyl. by M. Paul and Co., Dumbarton; 80 NHP, 640 IHP, 10.75 knots.

3.1890: Completed by Murray Brothers, Dumbarton (Yard No.12).
13.4.1890: Registered in the ownership of Joseph Russell, Port Glasgow as NUMBER TWELVE.
10.9.1890: Sold to William A. Grainger, Belfast.
18.9.1894: Renamed TEST.
4.2.1899: Sold to the Medway Navigation Co. Ltd., London.
6.12.1905: Sold to Frederick D. Bain trading as Bain, Son and Co., Portreath.
1.10.1915: Sold to John Ellis, Aberdeen.
22.8.1928: Transferred to Ellis and McHardy Ltd., Aberdeen.
17.12.1934: Sold to Monroe Brothers Ltd., Liverpool.
1.12.1936: Transferred to the Kyle Shipping Co. Ltd. (Monroe Brothers, managers), Liverpool.
19.7.1940: Sold to the Admiralty.
2.4.1941: Register closed.
By 5.1944: In use as a barge for ammunition storage at HMS VERNON, Portsmouth.
1.11.1946: Handed over to the Director of Supplies and Transport, presumably for disposal.

Plover manoeuvres into her discharge berth in the outer basin at Portreath. *[Paddy Bradley collection]*

Holme Wood at Bristol. *[J. and M. Clarkson]*

Test passing Anchor Wharf, Chatham following sale by Bains. At one time this 1890-built steamer carried Cunard's funnel and flew their flag whilst on charter for the seasonal trade between the Channel Isles and Liverpool. *[Nautical Photo Agency/National Maritime Museum N43935]*

A CENTURY OF SLUDGE DISPOSAL AT SEA

Craig J.M. Carter

Towards the end of the 19th century many municipal authorities were facing the problem of safe and hygienic disposal of sewage effluent, otherwise known as treated sludge. Some city authorities, including those of London, Glasgow and Manchester, came to the decision that disposal at sea using specially-designed ships was the best answer.

The opening of the Manchester Ship Canal in 1894 provided the outlet to the sea for the twin cities of Manchester and Salford and they were not slow to take advantage of the waterway. Salford Corporation established a large sewage treatment works on the bank of the Canal at Weaste and an order was placed with William Simons and Co. Ltd. of Renfrew for a twin-screw sludge vessel. Delivered in 1895, Simons yard number 324 was a steamer of 818 gross tons appropriately named *Salford*.

Meanwhile Manchester Corporation were pursuing their own plans, building an extensive treatment works on the Canal bank at Davyhulme and their Rivers Department went to the Vickers shipyard at Barrow-in-Furness for a sludge carrier of just under 1,000 gross tons. This vessel, yard number 262, was launched on 17th July 1897 and was given the name *Joseph Thompson* after the Chairman of the Rivers Committee. A twin-screw triple-expansion system provided the propulsion power.

Both these ships were soon making regular runs from Weaste and Davyhulme via the Ship Canal to an appointed deposit ground in Liverpool Bay. A round voyage, depending upon tides and canal traffic, could take up to 16 hours.

Salford continued her work until 1928 when she was sold for breaking up at Preston by Thos. W. Ward Ltd., but an order had already been placed with William Beardmore and Co. Ltd., of Dalmuir for her replacement. A much larger vessel of 1,170 gross tons this was a twin-screw steamer named *Salford City*. She was delivered in 1928.

In 1933, the *Joseph Thompson* was sold for breaking up but the Manchester Corporation Rivers Department had already placed an order for her replacement with Ferguson Brothers (Port Glasgow) Ltd. This steamer of 1,286 gross tons was delivered in 1933 and given the name *Mancunium*, the Roman name for Manchester. With her tall black funnel the *Mancunium* soon became a familiar sight in the Ship Canal and the Mersey. Sadly her career was cut short when, on 15th January 1941, she struck a mine and sank two miles north east of the Mersey

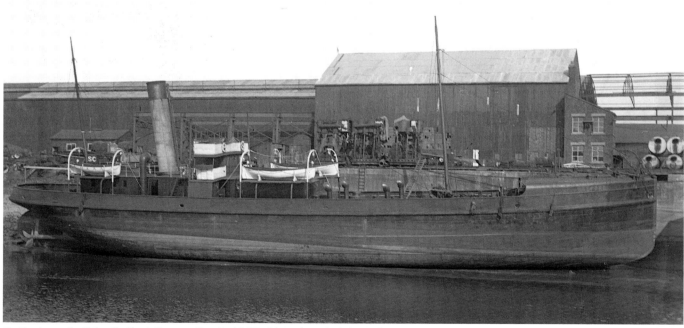

Salford was built for Salford Corporation in 1895. Note the whaleback forecastle and the two boats mounted alongside what is presumably a pump room. In the lower photograph *Salford* is awaiting demolition at Preston in 1928. *[Author's collection; J. and M. Clarkson]*

Manchester's first sludge disposal vessel, *Joseph Thompson* of 1897 (top). She was replaced in 1933. *[Author's collection]*

A loaded *Salford City* as built in 1928 sailing down the Manchester Ship Canal in post-war years (above) and sailing from Eastham in June 1967 after rebuilding, which included fitting diesel engines plus new superstructure, funnel and masts (right). The arms of Salford were displayed on her funnel. *[World Ship Society Ltd./J. and M. Clarkson]*

183

Mined in Liverpool Bay in 1941, *Mancunium* (1) of 1933 was the only member of the Manchester and Salford sewage fleet to be lost. *[Keith P. Lewis/Author's collection]*

Bar Light Vessel. The disaster put a considerable strain upon the work of the Rivers Department, as wartime restrictions made it impossible for an immediate replacement vessel to be ordered and for the next few years the *Salford City* helped with the work and the veteran *Shieldhall* (1,375/1910) was drafted in from Glasgow .

It was not until 1946 that Manchester Corporation was able to take delivery of *Mancunium* (2) from the yard of Ferguson Brothers (Port Glasgow) Ltd. At 1,334 gross tons she was similar but slightly larger than her predecessor and her general profile was the same.

By 1963 the *Salford City* was 35 years old and yet it was felt feasible to extend her life by re-engining with twin-screw diesel machinery. This was carried out by Manchester Drydocks Ltd., giving her another 13 years of service until her sale to Mayer Newman and Co. for breaking up at Fleetwood where she arrived on 24th June 1976.

In 1962 *Mancunium* (2) was also put into the hands of Manchester Drydocks Ltd. for re-engining with two six-cylinder Mirrlees National diesels, making her a much more economical vessel to operate. This extended her life with Manchester Corporation until 1970, when she was sold to Effluents Services Ltd. Transferred to work at Southampton she continued to bear the name *Mancunium* and remained registered at Manchester.

A new sludge vessel ordered from Ferguson Brothers (Port Glasgow) Ltd. by Manchester's Rivers Department was delivered in August 1968. Named *Percy Dawson* after Alderman S.P. Dawson, Chairman of the Rivers Committee, she was a twin-screw vessel of 1,285 gross tons with two six-cylinder turbo-charged engines giving a maximum speed of 13 knots. She could carry 1,500 tons of sewage slurry in four tanks together with 23 tons of noxious

Mancunium (2) of 1946 was a virtual repeat of her 1933 predecessor, and looked most anachronistic with her tall funnel and counter stern. She is seen at three stages in her career, first underway on the Manchester Ship Canal with a buff funnel with black top (opposite bottom), in 1972 after rebuilding with diesel engines and with Manchester's coat of arms on her new funnel (above), and further modified on the Solent on 5th August 1987 in the colours of Effluent Services Ltd. following her sale in 1970 (right). Still with her original name, she was broken up at Newport, Monmouthshire in January 1990. *[J. and M. Clarkson; World Ship Society Ltd.; Roy Fenton]*

Percy Dawson in 1972. In 1988 she was sold to Effluents Services Ltd. of Macclesfield and renamed *Haweswater*. A further sale in 1999 saw her go under the Greek flag as *Olympic*, as which she may be still afloat, as 'Lloyd's Register' have not been notified of her being scrapped. *[J. and M. Clarkson]*

fluid in a stainless steel tank specially installed for the carriage of industrial by-products. Accommodation for the crew of 13 was of a very high standard and included an officers' lounge, a comfortable dining room and tastefully fitted rooms for officers and men. The vessel was built under the supervision of Marker and Eccles of Manchester who had managed and operated the Manchester and Salford vessels for many years.

Two more sister ships were ordered for the joint Manchester-Salford operation in 1970. Once again Ferguson Brothers (Port Glasgow) Ltd. were the builders and they delivered *Gilbert J. Fowler* in 1971 and *Consortium 1* a year later. Sophisticated motor vessels of 1,548 gross tons with twin six-cylinder Mirrlees Blackstone engines giving a speed of 13 knots, they were provided with twin rudders, bow thrusters, VHF radio and radar. The crew of 16 enjoyed a high standard of accommodation. Nine tanks could be filled at Davyhulme through twin loading arms in about 35 minutes.

Consortium 1 took her name from a consortium of local councils in the Greater Manchester area which had joined together to deal with sewage sludge disposal. However, upon the formation of the North West Water Authority in 1974 the fleet of three vessels was taken into the new authority's ownership.

A major change in the operation occurred in 1987 with the completion of a pipeline from Weaste and Davyhulme to a new treatment plant at Sandon Dock, Liverpool. The sludge vessels made their last voyages along the Manchester Ship Canal, loading at Liverpool instead, thus considerably shortening their round voyages to the deposit ground.

Gilbert J. Fowler sails from Eastham in 1972. *[J. and M. Clarkson]*

Gilbert J. Fowler, renamed *Cape Georjean* and registered at La Paz, on the River Tyne in August 2000. *[H.S. Appleyard]*

Seen when new in 1972, *Consortium 1* was originally owned by the Bolton and District Joint Sewerage Board and Others, with management in the hands off Manchester Corporation's Rivers Department. On 1st April 1974 the owners of this and the sludge vessels previously owned by Manchester and Salford became the Middle Mersey Effluent Treatment Unit, a department of the newly-formed North West Water Authority. *[J. and M. Clarkson]*

In 1988 *Percy Dawson* was sold to Effluents Services. Ltd. and renamed *Haweswater* leaving the two newest vessels to carry on the work based at Sandon Dock. But in the mid 1990s new legislation meant that dumping sewage sludge at sea would have to cease. New plant at the Sandon Dock facility took over the work and the two remaining sister ships were offered for sale. A buyer was found for *Gilbert J. Fowler* in 2000 in the form of Ocean Maritime Ltd. Registered at La Paz under the flag of land-locked Bolivia, she was renamed *Cape Georjean* but was soon in trouble. In February 2001 she was reported to be detained on the Tyne with invalid safety certificates and no certificated master or mate. However, these problems were subsequently resolved and she sailed for South American waters. Briefly renamed *Tariq* in 2006, she was broken up in Pakistan later that year.

The sale of *Consortium 1* in 1999 was shrouded in mystery, and all that is known is that she went to buyers who put her under the flag of Honduras and registered her at San Lorenzo. Whether she is still afloat is open to question: 'Lloyd's Register' still includes her as *Consortium 1* but has not listed an owner since 2000.

Regarded by many as having a distasteful task, the sludge disposal vessels carried out 100 years of essential service to North West communities. The more recent vessels were kept spotlessly clean and boasted crew accommodation far better than many an ocean going ship.

Glasgow Corporation's *Shieldhall* was chartered by Manchester Corporation to help replace the Mancunium (1) following her loss in 1941. *Shieldhall* was built by William Beardmore and Co. Ltd., Glasgow in 1910 and was broken up at Port Glasgow in 1955. *[The Ballast Trust]*

PUTTING THE RECORD STRAIGHT

Letters, additions, amendments and photographs relating to features in any issues of 'Record' are welcomed. Letters may be lightly edited. Senders of e-mails are asked to include their postal address.

British Shipowners' Co. Ltd.

Malcolm Cooper's articles on this company generated much interest, and we are grateful to Ian Farquhar, Robert Langlois, Bill Schell, Barry Standerline and Bob Todd for the following comments and additions and to Kevin O'Donoghue for the accompanying photograph. Ed.
Sailing ship fleet list ('Record' 45):
No. 1. *Glenna* was built by Pile, Spence and Co., West Hartlepool (Yard No. 55).
No. 14. *British Statesman* had her register closed on 23.9.1885.
No. 25. *British General* was towed into Cardiff on 9.1.1908, dismasted during a voyage from Leixoes to Newport, Monmouthshire with a cargo of pitprops and was then sold for breaking up at Falmouth. Bill Schell notes that this does not preclude the possibility that the would-be breakers found it more profitable to sell her hull in one piece.
No. 37. *British Isles*, was still afloat as a lighter in 1934 when she was sold to Cia. Argentina de Nav. Mihanovich, Buenos Aires and re-named *Oceania*.
Steam ship fleet list ('Record' 46):
No. 2. *British Crown* (1): correct cylinder dimensions were: two x 28, 60 x 54 inches.
No. 3. *British Queen* (1) had engines by Palmer's Ship Building and Iron Co. Ltd., not Harland and Wolff, Belfast.

The photograph on page 112 was taken at Port Chalmers in July 1884, not at Lyttelton as first thought.
No. 12. *British Princess* (2) was photographed at Sydney as a Boer War transport (page 118).
No. 13. *British Prince* was launched on 21.10.1899.

P&O post war

The article in 'Record' 46 by Andrew Bell contains some statements that need clarification. The *Socotra* was not the forerunner of British India's 'C' class and *Cannanore* and *Coromandel* were not the first and second of the post-war batch. The 'C' class were a B.I. design developed just before the war, the first delivery being *Canara* in August 1942. The first post-war delivery was *Carpentaria*. The table shows details up to the *Coromandel*, all being built by Barclay, Curle. Yard numbers 687 to 692 were twin-screw, the remainder singe screw, all with Doxford engines.

Ship	Yard number	Delivered	Company
Canara	687	13.8.1942	British India
Chyebassa	688	24.12.1942	British India
Socotra	691	19.5.1943	P&O
Behar	692	8.1943	Hain
Chanda	695	12.7.1944	British India
Chupra	696	14.12.1944	British India
Carpentaria	709	21.4.1949	British India
Cannanore	712	5.7.1949	P&O
Coromandel	714	20.10.1949	P&O

The 1896-built cargo ship *British Trader* of the British Shipowners' Co. Ltd. at Antwerp, the European terminus of the Phoenix Line's fortnightly trans-Atlantic service for which she was chartered to Wilson Line. The sepia print has been crudely coloured to depict a red funnel with black top and blue band. She flies at her foremast head the flag of the USA, from where she has arrived. The photograph, taken between 1896 and 1906, shows at least four ocean-going sailing ships in the reach of the River Scheldt now known as the Oosterweel as well as a number of smaller sailing craft nearby. Flor van Otterdyk identifies the shot as being taken from the photographer's window, just south of the Bonaparte Dock and adjacent to the present pilotage building. *[Hugo Piéron-Loodts/ Kevin O'Donoghue collection]*

Canara of 1942, first of British India's 'C' class: see 'P&O post war'. *[FotoFlite incorporating Skyfotos]*

The photographs on page 77 are interesting in showing how the livery of a ship can alter her appearance, not always for the better. Whilst as *Salmara* she was quite a good-looking ship, the deletion of the white band round the hull which she had first carried as *Teesta* spoilt her sheer line. The final livery as *Strathloyal* shows her with that awful abomination, the P&O blue and white logo, which was foisted upon us in 1971, and ruined the appearance of every ship to which it was applied. The middle photograph shows her with the Crusader Line funnel.
TONY SMYTHE, 35 Avondale Road, Rayleigh, Essex SS6 8NJ

Strathloyal was broken up in 1978, not 1968. The WSS history of British India gives the vessel as sold to Jamal Enterprises Ltd on 19.11.77 with demolition commencing at Gadani Beach in January 1978.
RICHARD PRYDE, 4 Portlight Close, Mistley, Manningtree, Essex CO11 1UD

Barber Lines
Alan Dean is thanked for clarifying that Elder Dempster Lines had in fact purchased *Greystoke Castle*, *Penrith Castle* and *Muncaster Castle* in 1943, not in 1946 when wartime restrictions on renaming ships were lifted. Even though Mollers did not take control of James Chambers until the end of 1944, Chambers' decision to sell their remaining ships - presumably due to the high prices that the ships would have attracted in 1943 - indicates an existing degree of influence from Mollers whose approach to the business of ship owning was clearly short-term in nature.
　　Similarly the 1944 built *Greystoke Castle* and *Muncaster Castle,* which had entered Chambers' service in 1948 but in 1954 were chartered to Shaw Savill and Albion for five years as *Bardic* and *Gallic*, had by 1957 been sold

to Ben Line who renamed them *Benwyvis* and *Benrinnes* in 1959 when the charters had ended.
　　I take this opportunity to add that James Chambers had shortly before the Second World War taken delivery of three new ships, all of which were sunk in 1942: *Lancaster Castle* of 1937, *Lowther Castle* of 1937 and *Bolton Castle* of 1939.
MALCOLM CRANFIELD, 8 Foxcover Road, Heswall, Wirral L60 1YB

I enjoyed the article about Barber Lines A/S in 'Record' 45. When Barber Lines introduced their 'dramatic' new colour scheme, I recall that most mariners at the time considered it to be quite awful.
　　Many readers would have glanced at the photo of *Fernview* on page 48 without noticing her truncated bow, with 'flat front' complete with two round fairleads. The reason appeared to be the Bangkok port authority's regulation that the maximum overall length of a ship permitted to go up the river to Bangkok and turn was 565 feet, or 172.22 metres. When *Fernview* and *Fernlake* were lengthened (perhaps before they traded to Bangkok), they ended up a bit longer than that, so needed a short length removed at the bow to get back down to the 172.22 metre length to be able to trade to Bangkok. Photos of them as Wilhelmsen's *Texas* and *Tampa* respectively (with shortened bows) were published in the World Ship Society's history of Wilhelmsen on pages 236 and 235.
　　Most of the 'T's that were lengthened in 1970 and 1971 had the work carried out in Yokohama, and I recall seeing bits of ships floating around in the port there as tugs moved sections out of and into dry docks to carry out the work - the new colour scheme was hard to miss! These lengthenings did not exceed the 172.22 metre limit.
CAPTAIN MICHAEL PRYCE, 1 Edington Grove, Churton Park, Wellington 6137, New Zealand

The repainting of the three companies' vessels was an issue of importance. It was felt necessary to have a common colour scheme for all vessels in Barber Lines, since there would be a much more integrated service of the fleet operated jointly or individually by the three companies with a single management and operational company acting on behalf of Wilh. Wilhelmsen, Fearnley & Eger and A.F. Klaveness & Co.

A maritime paint company was involved as consultants and various colour schemes were considered. Eventually all three companies agreed on the orange hull and green superstructure, deck, rig and engine houses. The orange hulls were also considered to have safety advantages. As it turned out, the green colour was a pain in the neck. The bright fresh green colour quickly paled in tropical light, and the superstructure and decks looked awful when spots had to be repainted in fresh colours. Part of the reason was that Wilh. Wilhelmsen wanted to get away from the old style white hull band which was expensive to maintain (it was painted by brush or usually by rollers). Also note that Wilh Wilhelmsen started to repaint tankers and bulk carriers into the same orange and green colour scheme, but with Wilhelmsen's famous two light blue funnel bands. However, in 1977 when the series of six multi-purpose vessels were delivered, Wilhelmsen changed to a more reddish hull and white superstructure for liner vessels and later new ro-ro vessels. Tankers changed back to black hulls eventually - but without the famous white hull band. Supply ships were painted in two shades of orange and that scheme never changed for as long as Wilhelmsen had these vessels.

BJOERN PEDERSEN, Fiolveien 3A, N-1182 Oslo, Norway

BOSUN'S LOCKER

John Naylon 1931-2010

We were very sorry to learn in September of the death of John Naylon, regular contributor to 'Record', and indeed author of an article in our very first issue.

John was born in Bolton, Lancashire, the son of a railway engineer whose family's roots were in Southern Ireland. John read geography at Birmingham University, graduating in 1953, and going on to complete a PhD. His research, into irrigation systems in Spain, saw him spend long summers in the country and so immersing himself in its language and culture that he was often mistaken for a native Spanish speaker. He then took up a lectureship in geography at Keele University where he met his future wife Wenslie, who shared his love of horse riding. They lived in the village of Keele, where John became an active and committed parish councillor.

John's long and deep interest in the history of the sailing ship had both academic and practical aspects. As well as completing a number of immaculately researched articles, based on his extensive collection of written material and photographs, he also completed 14 voyages on the French sail training ship *Belem*, giving him a real insight into life on board a working square rigger. John had completed an article for 'Record' on the French bounty ships shortly before his sudden and unexpected death, and with the permission of his family we will be featuring this in a forthcoming edition. We offer our condolences to Wenslie and her family, and joining them in lamenting the loss of a man who could truly be called a scholar and a gentleman.

More on 44/02

Robert Langlois has written about this photograph of *Derfflinger*. To the 12 capital ships listed can be added *Markgraf* (raised 1937) and *Kronprinz Wilhelm* (raised 1938) according to John C. Taylor's 'German Warships of World War 1' (Ian Allan 1969). All but one of the 14 were broken up at Rosyth: *Friedrich der Grosse* (scrapped at Scapa). The wreck of a fifteenth, *König*, was 'broken up in 1962'. A sixteenth, *Baden*, had been beached at Scapa Flow on 21st June 1919, salved in July 1919 and expended as a gunnery target off Portsmouth on 16th August 1921. Reading how *Moltke* and its two tugs contrived to get tangled up with one of the Forth Bridge's supporting piers in 1927 reminded Robert of the cover of issue 43 of 'Shipping Wonders of the World', which depicts the *Kaiserin* passing underneath the Forth Bridge in charge of three tugs, one pulling and two secured to her sides (below). The picture is taken from the bridge looking down onto the battleship's upturned rust-coloured hull, with three propellers and twin rudders prominent. Taylor records that she was raised on 14th May 1936, so the picture must have taken later in May of that year. By then, perhaps, the salvors had realised that three tugs were needed to control such an unwieldy mass as an upturned battleship.

On Normandy beaches: Bill Schell has sent us for identification photographs taken immediately after the war on the Normandy beachhead. Bill points out that this one (above) is immediately identifiable as *Empire Bittern* (8,546/1902, scuttled 23rd July 1944) no other blockships had four masts.

47/01. The bow is missing from this vessel, but enough remains to be identified (below).

47/02. Although this ship has been badly damaged by storms, the serifed 'H' device on her funnel should help identification (above).

47/03. Note the number of 'visitors' on this ship: clearly nobody in authority cared who went aboard (below).

To conclude this issue we have a further three pictures for identification.

47/04. This photograph of a Holland Amerika liner (above) has nothing on the back but hopefully one of our Dutch readers will recognise her.

47/05. Above right we have a photograph by Grahame Farr taken at Bristol on 28th April 1935. The name, a long one, and port of registry can be seen but appear to have been painted over.

47/06. Our last picture (right) is of a liner possibly taken at Marseille, France as the publisher is H. Grimaud of Marseille. Not dated, the card is addressed to a Mr. Lankester at Tendring and is marked 'On Active Service' so one assumes it dates back to the First World War.

SOURCES AND ACKNOWLEDGEMENTS

We thank all who gave permission for their photographs to be used, and for help in finding photographs we are particularly grateful to Tony Smith, Jim McFaul and David Whiteside of the World Ship Photo Library; to Ian Farquhar, F.W. Hawks, Peter Newall, William Schell; and to David Hodge and Bob Todd of the National Maritime Museum; and other museums and institutions listed.

Research sources have included the *Registers* of William Schell and Tony Starke, 'Lloyd's Register', 'Lloyd's Confidential Index', 'Lloyd's Shipping Index', 'Lloyd's War Losses', 'Mercantile Navy Lists', 'Marine News', 'Sea Breezes' and 'Shipbuilding and Shipping Record'. Use of the facilities of the World Ship Society, the Guildhall Library, the National Archives and Lloyd's Register of Shipping and the help of Dr Malcolm Cooper are gratefully acknowledged. Particular thanks also to Heather Fenton for editorial and indexing work, and to Marion Clarkson for accountancy services.

Elder Dempster post war part 1
Books consulted include 'The Trade Makers: Elder Dempster in West Africa' by Professor Peter N. Davies; Allen and Unwin, London 1973 and 'The Elder Dempster Fleet History 1852-1985' by James E. Cowden and John O.C. Duffy; Mallett and Bell Publications, Norwich, 1986. Thanks also to James E. Cowden and Peter Newall.

Portreath and Bains
The author's are extremely grateful to Paddy Bradley, who allowed use of his wonderful collection of images of ships at Portreath, mostly taken by E. Bragg. The Percy Holman/ Tony Pawlyn collection comprises glass negatives of Holman's dry dock and foundry at Penzance, taken by Percy Holman, and currently lodged with the Royal Institution of Cornwall. Other photographs are from the authors' and editors' collections or as credited.

The text draws partly on two articles by the late Clive Carter: 'Coals to Portreath' in issue 1 of 'Archive', March 1994, and 'The Long Career of 'Rolling Reggie' in the 'Journal of the Trevithick Society', number 19, 1992. Also referred to was 'Portreath: Some Chapters in its History' by Michael Tangye, published by the author in 1978. Thanks also to Mike Grose for help with the history of Portreath and to Martin Benn for additional information on Bains' sailing ships.